MAD LOVE, MURDER & MAYHEM

Favorite English & Scottish Ballads

Illustrated Edition

JOSHUA HAMPTON

SEVEN CROWNS
PUBLISHING

Mad Love, Murder & Mayhem:
Favorite English & Scottish Ballads

First Edition: November 7, 2020

For more information about this book,
visit **www.JoshuaHampton.com**.

For My Wife

For Whom All My Ballads Are Written.

TABLE OF CONTENTS

Preface

The English and Scottish Popular Ballads, edited by Francis James Child, was published in ten parts, forming five large volumes, from 1882 to 1898. It contains three hundred and five distinct ballads, but the number of texts printed in full is much larger than this, for Professor Child's plan was to give every extant version of every ballad, [...] as well as exhaustive collations, elaborate bibliographies, an index of published ballad airs, a collection of tunes, and, in a word, all the apparatus necessary for the study of this kind of literature.

It is hoped [that this abridged collection] may be useful to the general reader and may lead those who feel a more particular interest in the subject to acquaint themselves at first hand with the full collection of texts and other apparatus in Mr. Child's admirable volumes.

Excerpted from the Preface of English and Scottish Popular Ballads, Student's Cambridge Edition, *1904*

A Note from the Author

Few things thrill writers more than the opportunity to discuss what inspires them. I'm no different, of course, hence the volume you hold now in hand. As they have with me, the English and Scottish ballads included in this book have moved countless novelists, poets, songwriters, filmmakers and more to build upon the timeless themes and narratives so perfectly anthologized by Harvard professor Francis James Child. These centuries-old tales have been lovingly passed down from generation to generation, providing the fabric with which countless beautiful works thereafter were created.

To those familiar with the ballads within these pages, I hope that you derive as much joy from their rediscovery as you did upon first finding them. Each song is a tome, brimful with secrets waiting to be revealed. To those for whom this volume serves as an introduction to the Child Ballads, you will soon discover it is no introduction at all. Though you may never have read them, you will remember them. Many you will recognize at once. Others may take a few readings. But you are sure to find comfort in their familiarity, as every line holds the history of us all.

FAVORITE ENGLISH & SCOTTISH BALLADS

Collected here are those Child Ballads that have become most widely known around the world, in both folk tradition and popular culture. As you read them, recite them aloud (or, better yet, sing them!) for they were written for the ears, not the eyes. And, please, seek out the recordings noted after each entry. Nothing can match the delight of hearing an olden song performed with reverence by a practiced voice, as was meant to be.

So go forth now and enjoy these ballads of kings, queens, serving men and maidens, sailors, spirits, demons and guardian angels; of redemption, betrayal, avengement and loss, and, of course, **Mad Love, Murder and Mayhem.**

— Joshua Hampton, May 2018

About the Text

The text of the ballads, but for a very few exceptions, is as it was originally presented by Child, including spelling errors and variances in the names of people and places. As Child often collected many variations of a single ballad, the letters to the left of each stanza identify the version of the ballad from which that stanza was taken in Child's original work. Where appropriate, this text also combines variants to more accurately recreate the versions of the ballads most popular among oral and musical traditions.

Listen As You Read

Visit Spotify for the audio companion to this book, a playlist with recordings of the Child Ballads by Led Zeppelin, Bob Dylan, 10,000 Maniacs, Lead Belly, Nick Cave and many more.

Search for Mad Love, Murder & Mayhem

Riddles Wisely Expounded

Child No. 1: Before agreeing to marry a maiden, a knight challenges her to answer several riddles. She does so easily, thus proving her wit, and the two are then happily wed.

1A.1   There was a lady of the North Country,
          Refrain: Lay the bent to the bonny broom
      And she had lovely daughters three.
          Refrain: Fa la la la, fa la la la la ra re

1A.2   There was a knight of noble worth
      Which also lived in the North.

1A.3   The knight, of courage stout and brave,
      A wife he did desire to have.

1A.4   He knocked at the ladie's gate
      One evening when it was late.

1A.5   The eldest sister let him in,
      And pin'd the door with a silver pin.

1A.6   The second sister she made his bed,
      And laid soft pillows under his head.

1A.7   The youngest daughter that same night,
      She went to bed to this young knight.

1A.8   And in the morning, when it was day,
      These words unto him she did say:

1A.9   'Now you have had your will,' quoth she,
         'I pray, sir knight, will you marry me?'

1A.10   The young brave knight to her replyed,
         'Thy suit, fair maid, shall not be deny'd.

1A.11   'If thou canst answer me questions three,
         This very day will I marry thee.'

1A.12   'Kind sir, in love, O then,' quoth she,
         'Tell me what your [three] questions be.'

1A.13   'O what is longer than the way,
         Or what is deeper than the sea?

1A.14   'Or what is louder than the horn,
         Or what is sharper than a thorn?

1A.15   'Or what is greener than the grass,
         Or what is worse than a woman was?'

1A.16   'O love is longer than the way,
         And hell is deeper than the sea.

1A.17   'And thunder is louder than the horn,
         And hunger is sharper than a thorn.

1A.18   'And poyson is greener than the grass,
         And the Devil is worse than woman was.'

1A.19   When she these questions answered had,
         The knight became exceeding glad.

1A.20   And having [truly] try'd her wit,
         He much commended her for it.

1A.21   And after, as it is verifi'd,
         He made of her his lovely bride.

3

1A.22   So now, fair maidens all, adieu,
            This song I dedicate to you.

1A.23   I wish that you may constant prove
            Unto the man that you do love.

BALLAD NOTES & HISTORY

This traditional English song dates back to at least 1450, and like most of the ballads Child collected, it exists in several variants. In the earliest surviving version of the song, *Inter Diabolus et Virgo* (Between the Devil and the Maiden), a demon threatens to abduct the maiden unless she can answer his riddles.

SELECTED RECORDINGS

Jean Redpath, *Riddles Wisely Expounded* (1982)

Anaïs Mitchell & Jefferson Hamer,
Riddles Wisely Expounded (Child 1) (2013)

Stray Hens, *Riddles Wisely Expounded
(Bonny Broom)* (2016)

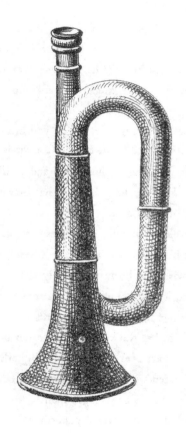

The Elfin Knight

Child No. 2: A clever girl wins a husband with her quick wit—when a knight challenges her to a series of impossible tasks, she matches his challenges with her own of equal difficulty, until the knight agrees to marry her.

2D.1   The Elfin knight stands on yon hill,
            Refrain: Blaw, blaw, blaw winds,
        blaw Blawing his horn loud and shrill.
            Refrain: And the wind has blawin my
                plaid awa

2A.2   He blowes it east, he blowes it west,
        He blowes it where he lyketh best.

2A.3   'I wish that horn were in my kist,
        Yea, and the knight in my armes two.'

2A.4   She had no sooner these words said,
        When that the knight came to her bed.

2A.5   'Thou art over young a maid,' quoth he,
        'Married with me thou il wouldst be.'

2A.6   'I have a sister younger than I,
        And she was married yesterday.'

2A.7   'Married with me if thou wouldst be,
        A courtesie thou must do to me.

2A.8   'For thou must shape a sark to me,
           Without any cut or heme,' quoth he.

2A.9   'Thou must shape it knife-and-sheerlesse,
           And also sue it needle-threedlesse.'

2A.10   'If that piece of courtesie I do to thee,
           Another thou must do to me.

2A.11   'I have an aiker of good ley-land,
           Which lyeth low by yon sea-strand.

2A.12   'For thou must eare it with thy horn,
           So thou must sow it with thy corn.

2A.13   'And bigg a cart of stone and lyme,
           Robin Redbreast he must trail it hame.

2A.14   'Thou must barn it in a mouse-holl,
           And thrash it into thy shoes soll.

2A.15   Thou must winnow it in thy looff,
           And also seck it in thy glove.

2A.16   'For thou must bring it over the sea,
           And thou must bring it dry home to me.

2A.17   En thou hast gotten thy turns well done,
           Then come to me and get thy sark then.'

2A.18   'I'l not quite my plaid for my life;
           It haps my seven bairns and my wife.'
              The wind shall not blow my plaid awa

2A.19   'My maidenhead I'l then keep still,
           Let the elphin knight do what he will.'
              The wind's not blown my plaid awa

BALLAD NOTES & HISTORY

Many believe *The Elfin Knight* to be an early variant of the popular ballad *Scarborough Fair*, perhaps most famously recorded by Simon & Garfunkel. Another well-known variant is *Whittingham Fair*, a song prevalent in northern England. There are several American versions as well, each of which differs greatly, including *My Father Had an Acre of Land*, *The Parsley Vine*, and *The Shirt of Lace*. The ballad provides the foundation for the melody and lyric of Bob Dylan's *Girl from the North Country*.

SELECTED RECORDINGS

Ewan MacColl & Peggy Seeger, *The Elfin Knight* (1956)

Martin Carthy, *Scarborough Fair* (1965)

Simon & Garfunkel, *Scarborough Fair/Canticle* (1966)

Eliza Carthy & Nancy Kerr, *Whittingham Fair* (1993)

Kate Rusby, *Elfin Knight* (2005)

Jean Luc Lenoir, *Elfin Knight* (2013)

Willie's Lady

Child No. 6: After Willie marries against his mother's wishes, she bewitches his pregnant wife with several charms that prevent her from giving birth. After attempts to bribe his mother fail, Willie turns to the advice of a household sprite who tells him to make a false baby of wax and then invite his mother to the christening. Fooled by the wax figure, the mother flies into a rage and reveals the details of her charms, which Willie quickly undoes, allowing his wife to finally deliver their baby.

6A.1   Willie has taen him oer the fame,
           He's woo'd a wife and brought her hame.

6A.2   He's woo'd her for her yellow hair,
           But his mother wrought her mickle care.

6A.3   And mickle dolour gard her dree,
           For lighter she can never be.

6A.4   But in her bower she sits wi pain,
           And Willie mourns oer her in vain.

6A.5   And to his mother he has gone,
           That vile rank witch of vilest kind.

6A.6   He says: 'My ladie has a cup,
           Wi gowd and silver set about.

6A.7 'This goodlie gift shall be your ain,
   And let her be lighter o her young bairn.'

6A.8 'Of her young bairn she'll neer be lighter,
   Nor in her bower to shine the brighter.

6A.9 'But she shall die and turn to clay,
   And you shall wed another may.'

6A.10 'Another may I'll never wed,
   Another may I'll neer bring home.'

6A.11 But sighing says that weary wight,
   'I wish my life were at an end.'

6A.12 'Ye doe [ye] unto your mother again,
   That vile rank witch of vilest kind.

6A.13 'And say your ladie has a steed,
   The like o'm's no in the lands of Leed.

6A.14 'For he [i]s golden shod before,
   And he [i]s golden shod behind.

6A.15 'And at ilka tet of that horse's main,
   There's a golden chess and a bell ringing.

6A.16 'This goodlie gift shall be your ain,
   And let me be lighter of my young bairn.'

6A.17 'O her young bairn she'll neer be lighter,
   Nor in her bower to shine the brighter.

6A.18 'But she shall die and turn to clay,
   And ye shall wed another may.'

6A.19 'Another may I['ll] never wed,
   Another may I['ll] neer bring hame.'

6A.20 But sighing said that weary wight,
   'I wish my life were at an end.'

6A.21 'Ye doe [ye] unto your mother again,
   That vile rank witch of vilest kind.

6A.22 'And say your ladie has a girdle,
   It's red gowd unto the middle.

6A.23 'And ay at every silver hem,
   Hangs fifty silver bells and ten.

6A.24 'That goodlie gift has be her ain,
   And let me be lighter of my young bairn.'

6A.25 'O her young bairn she's neer be lighter,
   Nor in her bower to shine the brighter.

6A.26 'But she shall die and turn to clay,
   And you shall wed another may.'

6A.27 'Another may I'll never wed,
   Another may I'll neer bring hame.'

6A.28 But sighing says that weary wight,
   'I wish my life were at an end.'

6A.29 Then out and spake the Belly Blind;
   He spake aye in good time.

6A.30 'Ye doe ye to the market place,
   And there ye buy a loaf o wax.

6A.31 'Ye shape it bairn and bairnly like,
   And in twa glassen een ye pit;

6A.32 'And bid her come to your boy's christening;
   Then notice weel what she shall do.

6A.33   'And do you stand a little fore bye,
And listen weel what she shall say.'

6A.34   'Oh wha has loosed the nine witch knots
That was amo that ladie's locks?

6A.35   'And wha has taen out the kaims of care
That hangs amo that ladie's hair?

6A.36   'And wha's taen down the bush o woodbine
That hang atween her bower and mine?

6A.37   'And wha has killd the master kid
That ran beneath that ladie's bed?

6A.38   'And wha has loosed her left-foot shee,
And lotten that ladie lighter be?'

6A.39   O Willie has loosed the nine witch knots
That was amo that ladie's locks.

6A.40   And Willie's taen out the kaims o care
That hang amo that ladie's hair.

6A.41   And Willie's taen down the bush o woodbine
That hang atween her bower and thine.

6A.42   And Willie has killed the master kid
That ran beneath that ladie's bed.

6A.43   And Willie has loosed her left-foot shee,
And letten his ladie lighter be.

6A.44   And now he's gotten a bonny young son,
And mickle grace be him upon.

BALLAD NOTES & HISTORY

Child's version of the ballad was written down from a recitation in Scotland around 1783. Other variations include Willie's wife being kept in labor for several years and dying whilst giving birth, with her sons born much older, swearing to avenge her.

SELECTED RECORDINGS

Martin Carthy, *Willie's Lady* (1976)

Lady Maisery, *Willie's Lady* (2011)

Anaïs Mitchell & Jefferson Hamer,
Willie's Lady (Child 6) (2013)

The Fair Flower of Northumberland

Child No. 9: A Scottish knight held prisoner by the English Earl of Northumberland persuades the Earl's daughter to free him, promising to marry her once he returns to Scotland. Yet when they reach his home, the knight reveals he already has a wife and children and bids the Earl's daughter return to England. She pleads with him to take her as his servant or to kill her, but he refuses. And so she returns home, disgraced but forgiven for falling for the knight's infamous Scottish charm.

9B.1   The provost's daughter went out a walking,
         Refrain: A may's love whiles is easy won

         She heard a poor prisoner making his moan,
         Refrain: And she was the fair flower of
         Northumberland.

9B.2   'If any lady would borrow me
         Refrain: Out into the prison strong,

         I would make her a lady of high degree,
         Refrain: For I am a great lord in
         fair Scotland.'

9B.3   She's done her to her father's bed-stock,
         Refrain: A may's love whiles is easy won

She's stolen the keys o many braw lock,
  Refrain: And she's loosd him out o the
  prison strong.

9B.4   She's done her to her father's stable,
  Refrain: A may's love whiles is easy won
She's taen out a steed that was both swift
  and able,
  Refrain: To carry them both to
  fair Scotland.

9B.5   O when they came to the Scottish cross,
  Refrain: A may's whiles is easy won
'Ye brazen-faced whore, light off o my horse,
  Refrain: And go get you back to
  Northumberland!'

9B.6   O when they came to the Scottish moor,
  Refrain: A may's love whiles is easy won
'Get off o my horse, you're a brazen-faced whore,
  Refrain: So go get you back to
  Northumberland!'

9B.7   'O pity on me, O pity,' said she,
  Refrain: 'O that my love was so easy won!
Have pity on me as I had upon thee,
  Refrain: When I loosd you out of the
  prison strong.'

9B.8   'O how can I have pity on thee?
  Refrain: O why was your love so easy won!

When I have a wife and children three
Refrain: More worthy than a'
Northumberland.'

9B.9 'Cook in your kitchen I will be,
Refrain: O that my love was so easy
won! And serve your lady most reverently,
Refrain: For I darena go back to
Northumberland.'

9B.10 'Cook in my kitchen you shall not be,
Refrain: Why was your love so easy won!
For I will have no such servants as thee,
Refrain: So get you back to
Northumberland.'

9B.11 But laith was he the lassie to tyne,
Refrain: A may's love whiles is easy won
He's hired an old horse and feed an old man,
Refrain: To carry her back to
Northumberland.

9B.12 O when she came her father before,
Refrain: A may's love whiles is easy won
She fell down on her knees so low
Refrain: For she was the fair flower of
Northumberland.

9B.13 'O daughter, O daughter, why was ye so bold,
Refrain: Or why was your love so easy won,

To be a Scottish whore in your fifteen year old?
Refrain: And you the fair flower of
Northumberland!'

9B.14   Her mother she gently on her did smile,
Refrain: O that her love was so easy won!
'She is not the first that the Scotts have beguild,
Refrain: But she's still the fair flower of
Northumberland.

9B.15   'She shanna want gold, she shanna want fee,
Refrain: Altho that her love was so easy won,
She shanna want gold to gain a man wi,
Refrain: And she's still the fair flower of
Northumberland.'

BALLAD NOTES & HISTORY

The earliest version of this ballad was called *Maiden Song* in a text dating to 1597. There are no variants of this ballad in languages other than English and Scots, though many of the elements appear in folk traditions around the world.

SELECTED RECORDINGS

The Exiles, *The Fair Flower of North Umberland* (1967)

Dick Gaughan, *The Fair Flower of North Umberland* (1972)

Martin Simpson, *The Fair Flower of North Umberland* (1984)

Alasdair Roberts, *The Fair Flower of North Umberland* (2018)

The Twa Sisters

Child No. 10: The oldest of the king's daughters takes her younger sister to the sea and drowns her. The dead sister is later found by a miller, who makes a viol using various parts of her body. Once completed, the instrument plays itself and sings the truth about her murder, implicating her sister.

10A.1   There were two sisters, they went playing,
        Refrain: With a hie downe downe a downe-a
    To see their father's ships come sayling in.
        Refrain: With a hy downe downe a downe-a

10A.2   And when they came unto the sea-brym,
    The elder did push the younger in.

10A.3   'O sister, O sister, take me by the gowne,
    And drawe me up upon the dry ground.'

10A.4   'O sister, O sister, that may not bee,
    Till salt and oatmeale grow both of a tree.'

10A.5   Somtymes she sanke, somtymes she swam,
    Until she came unto the mill-dam.

10A.6   The miller runne hastily downe the cliffe,
    And up he betook her withouten her life.

10A.7   What did he doe with her brest-bone?
    He made him a violl to play thereupon.

10A.8   What did he doe with her fingers so small?
        He made him peggs to his violl withall.

10A.9   What did he doe with her nose-ridge?
        Unto his violl he made him a bridge.

10A.10   What did he doe with her veynes so blew?
        He made him strings to his violl thereto.

10A.11   What did he doe with her eyes so bright?
        Upon his violl he played at first sight.

10A.12   What did he doe with her tongue so rough?
        Unto the violl it spake enough.

10A.13   What did he doe with her two shinnes?
        Unto the violl they danc'd Moll Syms.

10A.14   Then bespake the treble string,
        'O yonder is my father the king.'

10A.15   Then bespake the second string,
        'O yonder sitts my mother the queen.'

10A.16   And then bespake the strings all three,
        'O yonder is my sister that drowned mee.'

10A.17   'Now pay the miller for his payne,
        And let him bee gone in the divel's name.'

BALLAD NOTES & HISTORY

The Twa Sisters is first known to have appeared on a broadside in 1656 as *The Miller and the King's Daughter*. At least 21 English variants exist under several names, including *The Cruel Sister*, *The Wind and Rain*, and *Minnorie*. The melody was used by Bob Dylan as the foundation for *Percy's Song*.

SELECTED RECORDINGS

Willie Matheson, *Binnorie* (1951)

Ewan MacColl, *Minorie* (1956)

Frankie Armstrong, *The Two Sisters* (1972)

Martin Carthy & Dave Swarbrick, *The Bows of London* (1990)

Nancy Kerr & James Fagan, *The Berkshire Tragedy* (1997)

Martin Simpson, *The Wind and the Rain* (2009)

Alasdair Roberts, *The Two Sisters* (2010)

Emily Smith, *Twa Sisters* (2014)

Lord Randal

Child No. 12: Upon his return home, Lord Randal is confronted by his mother, who asks a series of questions about his doings. His answers are vague but ominous and she quickly gathers that he has been poisoned and is dying. Lord Randal at last admits she is right, and names his lover as his murderer.

12A.1   'O where ha you been, Lord Randal, my son?
      And where ha you been, my handsome
          young man?'
      'I ha been at the greenwood; mother, mak my
          bed soon,
      For I'm wearied wi hunting, and fain wad
          lie down.'

12A.2   'An what met ye there, Lord Randal, my son?
      An wha met you there, my handsome young man?'
      'O I met wi my true-love; mother, mak my
          bed soon,
      For I'm wearied wi huntin, an fain wad lie down.'

12A.3   'And what did she give you, Lord Randal, my son?
      And what did she give you, my handsome
          young man?'

'Eels fried in a pan; mother, mak my bed soon,
For I'm wearied wi huntin, and fain wad
 lie down.'

12A.4 'And wha gat your leavins, Lord Randal, my son?
And wha gat your leavins, my handsom
 young man?'

'My hawks and my hounds; mother, mak my
 bed soon,
For I'm wearied wi hunting, and fain wad
 lie down.'

12A.5 'And what becam of them, Lord Randal, my son?
And what becam of them, my handsome
 young man?'

'They stretched their legs out an died; mother,
 mak my bed soon,
For I'm wearied wi huntin, and fain wad
 lie down.'

12A.6 'O I fear you are poisoned, Lord Randal, my son!
I fear you are poisoned, my handsome
 young man!'

'O yes, I am poisoned; mother, mak my bed soon,
For I'm sick at the heart, and I fain wad
 lie down.'

12A.7 'What d'ye leave to your mother, Lord Randal,
 my son?

What d'ye leave to your mother, my handsome
    young man?'
'Four and twenty milk kye; mother, mak my
    bed soon,
For I'm sick at the heart, and I fain wad
    lie down.'

12A.8   'What d'ye leave to your sister, Lord Randal,
    my son?
What d'ye leave to your sister, my handsome
    young man?'
'My gold and my silver; mother, mak my
    bed soon,
For I'm sick at the heart, an I fain wad lie down.'

12A.9   'What d'ye leave to your brother, Lord Randal,
    my son?
What d'ye leave to your brother, my handsome
    young man?'
'My houses and my lands; mother, mak my
    bed soon,
For I'm sick at the heart, and I fain wad
    lie down.'

12A.10   'What d'ye leave to your true-love, Lord Randal,
    my son?
What d'ye leave to your true-love, my handsome
    young man?'

'I leave her hell and fire; mother, mak my
bed soon,
For I'm sick at the heart, and I fain wad
lie down.'

BALLAD NOTES & HISTORY

One of the most popular songs in Child's collection, this
Anglo-Scottish border ballad has variants found across
Europe in many languages including Irish, Danish, German,
Wendish and Swedish. An Italian version titled *Il
Testamento Dell'Avvelenato* (The Poisoned Man's Will)
dates as far back as 1629. Bob Dylan used the ballad's
question and answer structure as the foundation for his song
A Hard Rain's A-Gonna Fall. The poem is also alluded to
many times in J.D. Salinger's *The Catcher in the Rye*.

SELECTED RECORDINGS

Ewan MacColl, *Lord Randall* (1956)

Jean Ritchie, *Lord Randall* (1961)

Frank Proffitt, *Lord Randall* (1962)

Martin Carthy, *Lord Randall* (1972)

Dick Gaughan, *Lord Randal* (1977)

Peter Bellamy, *Lord Randall* (1985)

Alasdair Roberts, *Lord Ronald* (2005)

Lucy Ward, *Lord Randall* (2015)

The Cruel Mother

Child No. 20: A maiden gives birth to two babes alone in the woods, then murders and buries them in secret. Afterward on her walk home, she sees two young children playing and complements them on their beauty. The children tell her that they are her own murdered babes and that she will be damned for what she has done.

20C.1   She leaned her back unto a thorn,
   Refrain: Three, three, and three by three
 And there she has her two babes born.
   Refrain: Three, three, and thirty-three

20C.2   She took frae 'bout her ribbon-belt,
 And there she bound them hand and foot.

20C.3   She has taen out her wee pen-knife,
 And there she ended baith their life.

20C.4   She has howked a hole baith deep and wide,
 She has put them in baith side by side.

20C.5   She has covered them oer wi a marble stane,
 Thinking she would gang maiden hame.

20C.6   As she was walking by her father's castle wa,
 She saw twa pretty babes playing at the ba.

20C.7   'O bonnie babes, gin ye were mine,
 I would dress you up in satin fine.

20C.8   'O I would dress you in the silk,
         And wash you ay in morning milk.'

20C.9   'O cruel mother, we were thine,
         And thou made us to wear the twine.

20C.10   'O cursed mother, heaven's high,
         And that's where thou will neer win nigh.

20C.11   'O cursed mother, hell is deep,
         And there thou'll enter step by step.'

BALLAD NOTES & HISTORY

This ballad was first printed on a broadside dated 1638 and exists in a number of variants, including the verbosely titled *The Duke's Daughter's Cruelty: Or the Wonderful Apparition of two Infants whom she Murther'd and Buried in a Forrest, for to hide her Shame.* Variations of the ballad include *Greenwood Sidey* and *The Lady of York.*

SELECTED RECORDINGS

Ewan MacColl, *The Cruel Mother* (1956)

Shirley Collins, *The Cruel Mother* (1960)

Judy Collins, *Cruel Mother* (1964)

Joan Baez, *The Greenwood Side* (1967)

Martin Carthy, *Cruel Mother* (1971)

Alasdair Roberts, *The Cruel Mother* (2005)

10,000 Maniacs, *Greenwood Sidey* (2015)

The Three Ravens

Child No. 26: Three ravens discuss what they will eat for breakfast. One suggests they feast on a newly slain knight in a nearby field, but they find he is guarded by his loyal hounds and hawks, and is eventually beared away by his heartbroken lover.

26.1 There were three ravens sat on a tree,
     Refrain: Downe a downe, hay down, hay downe
  There were three ravens sat on a tree,
     Refrain: With a downe
  There were three ravens sat on a tree,
  They were as blacke as they might be.
     Refrain: With a downe derrie, derrie, derrie, downe, downe

26.2 The one of them said to his mate,
  'Where shall we our breakefast take?'

26.3 'Downe in yonder greene field,
  There lies a knight slain under his shield.

26.4 'His hounds they lie downe at his feete,
  So well they can their master keepe.

26.5 'His haukes they flie so eagerly,
  There's no fowle dare him come nie.'

26.6   Downe there comes a fallow doe,
        As great with yong as she might goe.

26.7   She lift up his bloudy hed,
        And kist his wounds that were so red.

26.8   She got him up upon her backe,
        And carried him to earthen lake.

26.9   She buried him before the prime,
        She was dead herselfe ere euen-song time.

26.10   God send every gentleman,
        Such haukes, such hounds, and such a leman.
        And there thou'll enter step by step.'

BALLAD NOTES & HISTORY

This English ballad was first printed in the songbook *Melismata* in 1611, but it is thought to be older than that. The Scottish variant, *Twa Corbies*, is sung to a different melody. Both are popular across Europe and the United States, with versions recorded in Russian, Polish, Hebrew, German, French, Danish, and several other languages. *The*

Three Ravens has also been featured in several works of literature and modern media, including the 2017 film *My Cousin Rachel* and the 1922 fantasy novel *The Worm Ouroboros*, a favorite of J.R.R. Tolkien and C.S. Lewis.

SELECTED RECORDINGS

Peter, Paul & Mary, *The Three Ravens* (1962)

Hamish Imlach, *Twa Corbies* (1967)

Steeleye Span, *Twa Corbies* (1970)

Sarah Leonard, *The Three Ravens* (1996)

Bert Jansch, *Twa Corbies* (2015)

King Henry

Child No. 32: While hunting, King Henry encounters a hideous woman who makes several demands of him—first that he serve her the meat of his horse, hounds and hawks, and finally that he bed her. He courteously obliges her every request and in the morning finds she has turned into a beautiful woman as a reward for his kindness.

32.1   Lat never a man a wooing wend
        That lacketh thingis three;
        A routh o gold, an open heart,
        Ay fu o charity.

32.2   As this I speak of King Henry,
        For he lay burd-alone;
        An he's doen him to a jelly hunt's ha,
        Was seven miles frae a town.

32.3   He chas'd the deer now him before,
        An the roe down by the den,
        Till the fattest buch in a' the flock
        King Henry he has slain.

32.4   O he has doen him to his ha,
        To make him beerly cheer;
        An in it came a griesly ghost,
        Steed stappin i the fleer.

32.5   Her head hat the reef-tree o the house,
        Her middle ye mot wel span;
        He's thrown to her his gay mantle,
        Says, 'Lady, hap your lingcan.'

32.6   Her teeth was a' like teather stakes,
        Her nose like club or mell;
        An I ken naething she 'peard to be,
        But the fiend that wons in hell.

32.7   'Some meat, some meat, ye King Henry,
        Some meat ye gie to me!'
        'An what meat's in this house, lady,
        An what ha I to gie?'
        'O ye do kill your berry-brown steed,
        An you bring him here to me.'

32.8   O whan he slew his berry-brown steed,
        Wow but his heart was sair!
        Shee eat him [a'] up, skin an bane,
        Left naething but hide an hair.

32.9   'Mair meat, mair meat, ye King Henry,
        Mair meat ye gi to me!'
        'An what meat's in this house, lady,
        An what ha I to gi?'
        'O ye do kill your good gray-hounds,
        An ye bring them a' to me.'

32.10   O whan he slew his good gray-hounds,
        Wow but his heart was sair!

She eat them a' up, skin an bane,
Left naething but hide an hair.

32.11 'Mair meat, mair meat, ye King Henry,
Mair meat ye gi to me!'
'An what meat's i this house, lady,
An what ha I to gi?'
'O ye do kill your gay gos-hawks,
An ye bring them here to me.'

32.12 O whan he slew his gay gos-hawks,
Wow but his heart was sair!
She eat them a' up, skin an bane,
Left naething but feathers bare.

32.13 'Some drink, some drink, now, King Henry,
Some drink ye bring to me!'
'O what drink's i this house, lady,
That you're nae welcome ti?'
'O ye sew up your horse's hide,
An bring in a drink to me.'

32.14 And he's sewd up the bloody hide,
A puncheon o wine put in;
She drank it a' up at a waught,
Left na ae drap ahin.

32.15 'A bed, a bed, now, King Henry,
A bed you mak to me!
For ye maun pu the heather green,
An mak a bed to me.'

32.16   O pu'd has he the heather green,
An made to her a bed,
An up has he taen his gay mantle,
An oer it has he spread.

32.17   'Tak aff your claiths, now, King Henry,
An lye down by my side!'
'O God forbid,' says King Henry,
'That ever the like betide;
That ever the fiend that wons in hell
Shoud streak down by my side.'
* * * * *

32.18   Whan night was gane, and day was come,
An the sun shone throw the ha,
The fairest lady that ever was seen
Lay atween him an the wa.

32.19   'O well is me!' says King Henry,
'How lang'll this last wi me?'
Then out it spake that fair lady,
'Even till the day you dee.

32.20   'For I've met wi mony a gentle knight
That's gien me sic a fill,
But never before wi a courteous knight
That ga me a' my will.'

BALLAD NOTES & HISTORY

This ballad has its origin in Norse and Celtic mythology. It closely parallels an episode in *The Saga of King Hlrofr Kraki.*

SELECTED RECORDINGS

Pete Seeger, *King Henry* (1966)

Steeleye Span, *King Henry* (1972)

Martin Carthy, *King Henry* (1974)

Mat Williams, *King Henry* (2012)

The Furrow Collective, *King Henry* (2014)

Alfred Deller, *King Henry* (2014)

Thomas Rymer

Child No. 37: While resting on the shore, a young minstrel encounters a beautiful woman astride a white horse. She reveals herself to be the Queen of Elfland then takes him upon her steed. She shows him the paths to heaven, hell and her own kingdom, before gifting him with fine clothing in exchange for seven years of servitude.

37C.1   True Thomas lay on Huntlie bank,
        A ferlie he spied wi' his ee,
        And there he saw a lady bright,
        Come riding down by the Eildon Tree.

37C.2   Her shirt was o the grass-green silk,
        Her mantle o the velvet fyne,
        At ilka tett of her horse's mane
        Hang fifty siller bells and nine.

37C.3   True Thomas, he pulld aff his cap,
        And louted low down to his knee:
        'All hail, thou mighty Queen of Heaven!
        For thy peer on earth I never did see.'

37C.4   'O no, O no, Thomas,' she said,
        "That name does not belang to me;
        I am but the queen of fair Elfland,
        That am hither come to visit thee.

37C.5   'Harp and carp, Thomas,' she said,
         'Harp and carp along wi me,
         And if ye dare to kiss my lips,
         Sure of your bodie I will be.'

37C.6   'Betide me weal, betide me woe,
         That weird shall never daunton me;'
         Syne he has kissed her rosy lips,
         All underneath the Eildon Tree.

37C.7   'Now, ye maun go wi me,' she said,
         'True Thomas, ye maun go wi me,
         And ye maun serve me seven years,
         Thro weal or woe, as may chance to be.'

37C.8   She mounted on her milk-white steed,
         She's taen True Thomas up behind,
         And aye wheneer her bridle rung,
         The steed flew swifter than the wind.

37C.9   O they rade on, and farther on,
         The steed gaed swifter than the wind,
         Untill they reached a desart wide,
         And living land was left behind.

37C.10   'Light down, light down, now, True Thomas,
         And lean your head upon my knee;
         Abide and rest a little space,
         And I will shew you ferlies three.

37C.11   'O see ye not yon narrow road,
         So thick beset with thorns and briers?

That is the path of righteousness,
Tho after it but few enquires.

37C.12 'And see not ye that braid braid road,
That lies across that lily leven?
That is the path of wickedness,
Tho some call it the road to heaven.

37C.13 'And see not ye that bonny road,
That winds about the fernie brae?
That is the road to fair Elfland,
Where thou and I this night maun gae.

37C.14 'But, Thomas, ye maun hold your tongue,
Whatever ye may hear or see,
For, if you speak word in Elflyn land,
Ye'll neer get back to your ain countrie.'

37C.15 O they rade on, and farther on,
And they waded thro rivers aboon the knee,
And they saw neither sun nor moon,
But they heard the roaring of the sea.

37C.16 It was mirk mirk night, and there was nae
        stern light,
And they waded thro red blude to the knee;
For a' the blude that's shed on earth
Rins thro the springs o that countrie.

37C.17 Syne they came on to a garden green,
And she pu'd an apple frae a tree:

'Take this for thy wages, True Thomas,
It will give the tongue that can never lie.'

37C.18　'My tongue is mine ain,' True Thomas said;
'A gudely gift ye wad gie to me!
I neither dought to buy nor sell,
At fair or tryst where I may be.

37C.19　'I dought neither speak to prince or peer,
Nor ask of grace from fair ladye:'
'Now hold thy peace,' the lady said,
'For as I say, so must it be.'

37C.20　He has gotten a coat of the even cloth,
And a pair of shoes of velvet green,
And till seven years were gane and past
True Thomas on earth was never seen.

BALLAD NOTES & HISTORY

Thomas Rhymer was a real historical figure, Sir Thomas
de Ercildoun, a Scottish laird and reputed prophet. The
ballad was first printed in Sir Walter Scott's *The Minstrelsy
of the Scottish Border* in 1803. Scott used as his source a

manuscript by famed ballad collector Anna Gordon, also known as Mrs. Brown of Falkland.

SELECTED RECORDINGS

Ewan MacColl, *Thomas Rhymer* (1956)

Hermes Nye, *Thomas the Rhymer* (1957)

Steeleye Span, *Thomas the Rhymer* (1974)

Mary Macmaster, *True Thomas* (1991)

Archie Fisher, *Thomas the Rhymer* (2017)

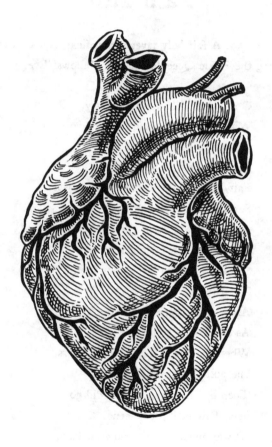

Tam Lin

Child No. 39: A fair lady saves a charming scoundrel from becoming the Fairie Queen's tithe on Hallows' Eve.

39D.1   O all you ladies young and gay,
       Who are so sweet and fair,
       Do not go into Chaster's wood,
       For Tomlin will be there.

39D.2   Fair Margret sat in her bonny bower,
       Sewing her silken seam,
       And wished to be in Chaster's wood,
       Among the leaves so green.

39D.3   She let her seam fall to her foot,
       The needle to her toe,
       And she has gone to Chaster's wood,
       As fast as she could go.

39D.4   When she began to pull the flowers,
       She pulld both red and green;
       Then by did come, and by did go,
       Said, Fair maid, let aleene.

39D.5   'O why pluck you the flowers, lady,
       Or why climb you the tree?
       Or why come ye to Chaster's wood
       Without the leave of me?'

39D.6   'O I will pull the flowers,' she said,
         'Or I will break the tree,
         For Chaster's wood it is my own,
         I'll no ask leave at thee.'

39D.7   He took her by the milk-white hand,
         And by the grass green sleeve,
         And laid her low down on the flowers,
         At her he asked no leave.

39D.8   The lady blushed, and sourly frowned,
         And she did think great shame;
         Says, 'if you are a gentleman,
         You will tell me your name.'

39D.9   'First they did call me Jack,' he said,
         'And then they called me John,
         But since I lived in the fairy court
         Tomlin has always been my name.

39D.10   'So do not pluck that flower, lady,
         That has these pimples gray;
         They would destroy the bonny babe
         That we've got in our play.'

39D.11   'O tell me, Tomlin,' she said,
         'And tell it to me soon,
         Was you ever at good church-door,
         Or got you christendoom?'

39D.12   'O I have been at good church-door,
         And aff her yetts within;

I was the Laird of Foulis's son,
The heir of all this land.

39D.13 'But it fell once upon a day,
As hunting I did ride,
As I rode east and west yon hill
There woe did me betide.

39D.14 'O drowsy, drowsy as I was!
Dead sleep upon me fell;
The Queen of Fairies she was there,
And took me to hersell.

39D.15 'The Elfins is a pretty place,
In which I love to dwell,
But yet at every seven years' end
The last here goes to hell;
And as I am ane o flesh and blood,
I fear the next be mysell.

39D.16 'The morn at even is Halloween;
Our fairy court will ride,
Throw England and Scotland both,
Throw al the world wide;
And if ye would me borrow,
At Rides Cross ye may bide.

39D.17 'You may go into the Miles Moss,
Between twelve hours and one;
Take holy water in your hand,
And cast a compass round.

39D.18 'The first court that comes along,
   You'll let them all pass by;
   The next court that comes along,
   Salute them reverently.

39D.19 'The next court that comes along
   Is clad in robes of green,
   And it's the head court of them all,
   For in it rides the queen.

39D.20 'And I upon a milk-white steed,
   With a gold star in my crown;
   Because I am an earthly man
   I'm next to the queen in renown.

39D.21 'Then seize upon me with a spring,
   Then to the ground I'll fa,
   And then you'll hear a rueful cry
   That Tomlin is awa.

39D.22 'Then I'll grow in your arms two
   Like to a savage wild;
   But hold me fast, let me not go,
   I'm father of your child.

39D.23 'I'll grow into your arms two
   Like an adder or a snake;
   But hold me fast, let me not go,
   I'll be your earthly maick.

39D.24 'I'll grow into your arms two
   Like iron in strong fire;

But hold me fast, let me not go,
Then you'll have your desire.'

39D.25 She rid down to Miles Cross,
Between twelve hours and one,
Took holy water in her hand,
And cast a compass round.

39D.26 The first court that came along,
She let them all pass by;
The next court that came along
Saluted reverently.

39D.27 The next court that came along
Were clad in robes of green,
When Tomlin, on a milk-white steed,
She saw ride with the queen.

39D.28 She seized him in her arms two,
He to the ground did fa,
And then she heard a ruefull cry
'Tomlin is now awa.'

39D.29 He grew into her arms two
Like to a savage wild;
She held him fast, let him not go,
The father of her child.

39D.30 He grew into her arms two
Like an adder or a snake;
She held him fast, let him not go,
He was her earthly maick.

39D.31   He grew into her arms two
           Like iron in hot fire;
           She held him fast, let him not go,
           He was her heart's desire.

39D.32   Then sounded out throw elphin court,
           With a loud shout and a cry,
           That the pretty maid of Chaster's wood
           That day had caught her prey.

39D.33   'O stay, Tomlin,' cried Elphin Queen,
           'Till I pay you your fee;'
           'His father has lands and rents enough,
           He wants no fee from thee.'

39D.34   'O had I known at early morn
           Tomlin would from me gone,
           I would have taken out his heart of flesh
           Put in a heart of stone.'

BALLAD NOTES & HISTORY

This English ballad dates to at least 1549 and is known
by many names, including *Tamlane, Tamlin, Tomlin, Tam*

Lien, *Tam-a-Line*, *Tam Lyn* and *Tam Lane*. Child included fourteen variants in his collection. The ballad was the inspiration for the 1970 film *Tam-Lin* directed by Roddy McDowall and starring Ava Gardner and Ian McShane.

SELECTED RECORDINGS

Fairport Convention, *Tam Lin* (1968)

A.L. Lloyd, *Tamlyn* (*Young Tambling*) (1972)

Frankie Armstrong, *Tam Lin* (1976)

Steeleye Span, *Tam Lin* (1991)

Bill Jones, *The Tale of Tam Lin* (2001)

Pentangle, *Tam Lin* (2007)

Anaïs Mitchell & Jefferson Hamer,
Tam Lin (Child 39) (2013)

Proud Lady Margaret

Child No. 47: A knight comes to a maiden's castle to woo her, but she is doubtful of his high rank due to his poor manner of dress. She challenges him with several riddles, which he answers, winning her courtship. He then reveals he is the ghost of her brother lost at sea, and warns her to curb her haughty ways.

47B.1　　There was a knight, in a summer's night,
　　　　　Appeard in a lady's hall,
　　　　　As she was walking up and down,
　　　　　Looking oer her castle wall.

47B.2　　'God make you safe and free, fair maid,
　　　　　God make you safe and free!'
　　　　　'O sae fa you, ye courteous knight,
　　　　　What are your wills wi me?'

47B.3　　'My wills wi you are not sma, lady,
　　　　　My wills wi you nae sma,
　　　　　And since there's nane your bower within,
　　　　　Ye'se hae my secrets a'.

47B.4　　'For here am I a courtier,
　　　　　A courtier come to thee,
　　　　　And if ye winna grant your love,
　　　　　All for your sake I'll dee.'

47B.5 'If that ye dee for me, sir knight,
  Few for you will make meen;
  For mony gude lord's done the same,
  Their graves are growing green.'

47B.6 'O winna ye pity me, fair maid,
  O winna ye pity me?
  O winna ye pity a courteous knight,
  Whose love is laid on thee?'

47B.7 'Ye say ye are a courteous knight,
  But I think ye are nane;
  I think ye're but a millar bred,
  By the colour o your claithing.

47B.8 'You seem to be some false young man,
  You wear your hat sae wide;
  You seem to be some false young man,
  You wear your boots sae side.'

47B.9 'Indeed I am a courteous knight,
  And of great pedigree;
  Nae knight did mair for a lady bright
  Than I will do for thee.

47B.10 'O I'll put smiths in your smithy,
  To shoe for you a steed,
  And I'll put tailors in your bower,
  To make for you a weed.

47B.11 'I will put cooks in your kitchen,
  And butlers in your ha,

And on the tap o yourn father's castle
I'll big gude corn and saw.'

47B.12 'If ye be a courteous knight,
As I trust not ye be,
Ye'll answer some o the sma questions
That I will ask at thee.

47B.13 'What is the fairest flower, tell me,
That grows in mire or dale?
Likewise, which is the sweetest bird
Sings next the nightingale?
Or what's the finest thing,' she says,
'That king or queen can wile?'

47B.14 'The primrose is the fairest flower
That grows in mire or dale;
The mavis is the sweetest bird
Next to the nightingale;
And yellow gowd's the finest thing
That king or queen can wale.

47B.15 'Ye hae asked many questions, lady,
I've you as many told;'
'But how many pennies round
Make a hundred pounds in gold?

47B.16 'How many of the small fishes
Do swim the salt seas round?
Or what's the seemliest sight you'll see
Into a May morning?'

* * * * *

47B.17 'Berry-brown ale and a birken speal,
    And wine in a horn green;
    A milk-white lace in a fair maid's dress
    Looks gay in a May morning.'

47B.18 'Mony's the questions I've askd at thee,
    And ye've answerd them a';
    Ye are mine, and I am thine,
    Amo the sheets sae sma.

47B.19 'You may be my match, kind sir,
    You may be my match and more;
    There neer was ane came sic a length
    Wi my father's heir before.

47B.20 'My father's lord o nine castles,
    My mother she's lady ower three,
    And there is nane to heir them all,
    No never a ane but me;
    Unless it be Willie, my ae brother,
    But he's far ayont the sea.'

47B.21 'If your father's laird o nine castles,
    Your mother lady ower three,
    I am Willie your ae brother,
    Was far beyond the sea.'

47B.22 'If ye be Willie, my ae brother,
    As I doubt sair ye be,

But if it's true ye tell me now,
This night I'll gang wi thee.'

47B.23 'Ye've ower ill washen feet, Janet,
And ower ill washen hands,
And ower coarse robes on your body,
Alang wi me to gang.

47B.24 'The worms they are my bed-fellows,
And the cauld clay my sheet,
And the higher that the wind does blaw,
The sounder I do sleep.

47B.25 'My body's buried in Dumfermline,
And far beyond the sea,
But day nor night nae rest coud get,
All for the pride o thee.

47B.26 'Leave aff your pride, jelly Janet,' he says,
'Use it not ony mair;
Or when ye come where I hae been
You will repent it sair.

47B.27 'Cast aff, cast aff, sister,' he says,
'The gowd lace frae your crown;
For if ye gang where I hae been,
Ye'll wear it laigher down.

47B.28 'When ye're in the gude church set,
The gowd pins in your hair,
Ye take mair delight in your feckless dress
Than ye do in your morning prayer.

47B.29 'And when ye walk in the church-yard,
And in your dress are seen,
There is nae lady that sees your face
But wishes your grave were green.

47B.30 'You're straight and tall, handsome withall,
But your pride owergoes your wit,
But if ye do not your ways refrain,
In Pirie's chair ye'll sit.

47B.31 'In Pirie's chair you'll sit, I say,
The lowest seat o hell;
If ye do not amend your ways,
It's there that ye must dwell.'

47B.32 Wi that he vanishd frae her sight,
Wi the twinkling o an eye;
Naething mair the lady saw
But the gloomy clouds and sky.

BALLAD NOTES & HISTORY

This variant is based on a version Sir Walter Scott
included in his collection *The Minstrelsy of the Scottish*

Border. It was communicated to Scott by a music-seller in Edinburgh who learned it from his mother.

SELECTED RECORDINGS

Ewan MacColl, *Proud Lady Margaret* (1964)

Pete & Chris Coe, *Proud Lady Margaret* (1975)

The Twa Brothers

Child No. 49: Two brothers are wrestling when one is unintentionally wounded by the other's knife. The dying brother tells the other to bury him, then gives him a list of excuses to tell their family to hide the sad truth of his untimely end. Only his true love is to be told the truth.

49A.1   There were twa brethren in the north,
    They went to the school thegither;
    The one unto the other said,
    Will you try a warsle afore?

49A.2   They warsled up, they warsled down,
    Till Sir John fell to the ground,
    And there was a knife in Sir Willie's pouch,
    Gied him a deadlie wound.

49A.3   'Oh brither dear, take me on your back,
    Carry me to yon burn clear,
    And wash the blood from off my wound,
    And it will bleed nae mair.'

49A.4   He took him up upon his back,
    Carried him to yon burn clear,
    And washd the blood from off his wound,
    But aye it bled the mair.

49A.5 'Oh brither dear, take me on your back,
   Carry me to yon kirk-yard,
   And dig a grave baith wide and deep,
   And lay my body there.'

49A.6 He's taen him up upon his back,
   Carried him to yon kirk-yard,
   And dug a grave baith deep and wide,
   And laid his body there.

49A.7 'But what will I say to my father dear,
   Gin he chance to say, Willie, whar's John?'
   'Oh say that he's to England gone,
   To buy him a cask of wine.'

49A.8 'And what will I say to my mother dear,
   Gin she chance to say, Willie, whar's John?'
   'Oh say that he's to England gone,
   To buy her a new silk gown.'

49A.9 'And what will I say to my sister dear,
   Gin she chance to say, Willie, whar's John?'
   'Oh say that he's to England gone,
   To buy her a wedding ring.'

49A.10 'But what will I say to her you loe dear,
   Gin she cry, Why tarries my John?'
   'Oh tell her I lie in Kirk-land fair,
   And home again will never come.'

69

BALLAD NOTES & HISTORY

This ballad is Scottish in origin and dates to the early 1800's. There are many variants, including several where one brother intentionally stabs the other and the dying brother's true love charms him out of his grave.

SELECTED RECORDINGS

Hobart Smith, *The Two Brothers*
(The Little Schoolboy) (1942)

Ewan MacColl, *The Two Brothers* (1961)

Peter Bellamy, *Two Pretty Boys* (1969)

Nic Jones, *The Two Brothers* (1971)

Lizzie Higgins, *The Twa Brothers* (1975)

Silly Wizard, *The Twa Brothers* (1978)

Jean Redpath, *The Twa Brothers* (1979)

Alasdair Roberts, *The Two Brothers* (2005)

Sir Patrick Spens

Child No. 58: The king calls for a great sailor to command a ship for a royal errand. He is told that Sir Patrick Spens is the best upon the sea, and so the king sends for him. However, Spens is hesitant to go, fearing raging tides and a winter storm, but ultimately he acquiesces to his king's request. In the end he was right to be wary—he is killed when his ship sinks on the voyage.

58A.1   The king sits in Dumferling toune,
         Drinking the blude-reid wine:
         'O whar will I get guid sailor,
         To sail this schip of mine?'

58A.2   Up and spak an eldern knicht,
         Sat at the kings richt kne:
         'Sir Patrick Spence is the best sailor
         That sails upon the se.'

58A.3   The king has written a braid letter,
         And signd it wi his hand,
         And sent it to Sir Patrick Spence,
         Was walking on the sand.

58A.4   The first line that Sir Patrick red,
         A loud lauch lauched he;

The next line that Sir Patrick red,
The teir blinded his ee.

58A.5   'O wha is this has don this deid,
This ill deid don to me,
To send me out this time o' the yeir,
To sail upon the se!

58A.6   'Mak hast, mak haste, my mirry men all,
Our guid schip sails the morne:'
'O say na sae, my master deir,
For I feir a deadlie storme.

58A.7   'Late late yestreen I saw the new moone,
Wi the auld moone in hir arme,
And I feir, I feir, my deir master,
That we will cum to harme.'

58A.8   O our Scots nables wer richt laith
To weet their cork-heild schoone;
Bot lang owre a' the play wer playd,
Their hats they swam aboone.

58A.9   O lang, lang may their ladies sit,
Wi thair fans into their hand,
Or eir they se Sir Patrick Spence
Cum sailing to the land.

58A.10 O lang, lang may the ladies stand,
Wi thair gold kems in their hair,
Waiting for thair ain deir lords,
For they'll se thame na mair.

73

58A.11   Haf owre, haf owre to Aberdour,
           It's fiftie fadom deip,
           And thair lies guid Sir Patrick Spence,
           Wi the Scots lords at his feit.

BALLAD NOTES & HISTORY

Child collected eighteen versions of *Sir Patrick Spens*, and it has remained one of the most anthologized British ballads. It was first published in *Reliques of Ancient English Poetry* by Bishop Thomas Percy in 1765. There is no "Patrick Spens" found in the historical record of the time, however some believe the name to be a variation of Sir Patrick Vans Barnbarroch, a Scottish diplomat who accompanied James VI on a storm-laden voyage in 1589.

SELECTED RECORDINGS

Ewan MacColl, *Sir Patrick Spens* (1956)

Fairport Convention, *Sir Patrick Spens* (1969)

Nic Jones, *Sir Patrick Spens* (1970)

Peter Bellamy, Sir Patrick Spens (1982)

Martin Carthy, Sir Patrick Spens (1998)

Martin Simpson, Sir Patrick Spens (2009)

Anaïs Mitchell & Jefferson Hamer,
Sir Patrick Spens (Child 58) (2013)

Michiel Schrey, *Sir Patrick Spens* (2013)

Fair Annie

Child No. 62: Annie, a lord's mistress who has born him seven sons and is pregnant with the eighth, is made to meet his bride-to-be. She welcomes the bride but laments her own fate, even wishing her sons would turn into rabbits and she into a hound to chase them. The bride then reveals that she is Annie's sister and promises to gift her a dowry of seven ships loaded with gold so that Annie can marry the lord and be happy.

62A.1 It's narrow, narrow, make your bed,
   And learn to lie your lane;
   For I'm ga'n oer the sea, Fair Annie,
   A braw bride to bring hame.
   Wi her I will get gowd and gear;
   Wi you I neer got nane.

62A.2 'But wha will bake my bridal bread,
   Or brew my bridal ale?
   And wha will welcome my brisk bride,
   That I bring oer the dale?'

62A.3 'It's I will bake your bridal bread,
   And brew your bridal ale,
   And I will welcome your brisk bride,
   That you bring oer the dale.'

62A.4   'But she that welcomes my brisk bride
         Maun gang like maiden fair;
         She maun lace on her robe sae jimp,
         And braid her yellow hair.'

62A.5   'But how can I gang maiden-like,
         When maiden I am nane?
         Have I not born seven sons to thee,
         And am with child again?'

62A.6   She's taen her young son in her arms,
         Another in her hand,
         And she's up to the highest tower,
         To see him come to land.

62A.7   'Come up, come up, my eldest son,
         And look oer yon sea-strand,
         And see your father's new-come bride,
         Before she come to land.'

62A.8   'Come down, come down, my mother dear,
         Come frae the castle wa!
         I fear, if langer ye stand there,
         Ye'll let yoursell down fa.'

62A.9   And she gaed down, and farther down,
         Her love's ship for to see,
         And the topmast and the mainmast
         Shone like the silver free.

62A.10   And she's gane down, and farther down,
         The bride's ship to behold,

And the topmast and the mainmast
They shone just like the gold.

62A.11　She's taen her seven sons in her hand,
I wot she didna fail;
She met Lord Thomas and his bride,
As they came oer the dale.

62A.12　'You're welcome to your house, Lord Thomas,
You're welcome to your land;
You're welcome with your fair ladye,
That you lead by the hand.

62A.13　'You're welcome to your ha's, ladye,
Your welcome to your bowers;
You're welcome to your hame, ladye,
For a' that's here is yours.'

62A.14　'I thank thee, Annie; I thank thee, Annie,
Sae dearly as I thank thee;
You're the likest to my sister Annie,
That ever I did see.

62A.15　'There came a knight out oer the sea,
And steald my sister away;
The shame scoup in his company,
And land whereer he gae!'

62A.16　She hang ae napkin at the door,
Another in the ha,
And a' to wipe the trickling tears,
Sae fast as they did fa.

62A.17   And aye she served the lang tables,
With white bread and with wine,
And aye she drank the wan water,
To had her colour fine.

62A.18   And aye she served the lang tables,
With white bread and with brown;
And ay she turned her round about,
Sae fast the tears fell down.

62A.19   And he's taen down the silk napkin,
Hung on a silver pin,
And aye he wipes the tear trickling
A' down her cheek and chin.

62A.20   And aye he turn'd him round about,
And smiled amang his men;
Says, Like ye best the old ladye,
Or her that's new come hame?

62A.21   When bells were rung, and mass was sung,
And a' men bound to bed,
Lord Thomas and his new-come bride
To their chamber they were gaed.

62A.22   Annie made her bed a little forbye,
To hear what they might say;
'And ever alas!' Fair Annie cried,
'That I should see this day!

62A.23   'Gin my seven sons were seven young rats,
Running on the castle wa,

And I were a grew cat mysell,
I soon would worry them a'.

62A.24   'Gin my seven sons were seven young hares,
Running oer yon lilly lee,
And I were a grew hound mysell,
Soon worried they a' should be.'

62A.25   And wae and sad Fair Annie sat,
And drearie was her sang,
And ever, as she sobbd and grat,
'Wae to the man that did the wrang!'

62A.26   'My gown is on,' said the new-come bride,
'My shoes are on my feet,
And I will to Fair Annie's chamber,
And see what gars her greet.

62A.27   'What ails ye, what ails ye, Fair Annie,
That ye make sic a moan?
Has your wine barrels cast the girds,
Or is your white bread gone?

62A.28   'O wha was't was your father, Annie,
Or wha was't was your mother?
And had ye ony sister, Annie,
Or had ye ony brother?'

62A.29   'The Earl of Wemyss was my father,
The Countess of Wemyss my mother;
And a' the folk about the house
To me were sister and brother.'

62A.30 'If the Earl of Wemyss was your father,
I wot sae was he mine;
And it shall not be for lack o gowd
That ye your love sall tyne.

62A.31 'For I have seven ships o mine ain,
A' loaded to the brim,
And I will gie them a' to thee,
Wi four to thine eldest son:
But thanks to a' the powers in heaven
That I gae maiden hame!'

BALLAD NOTES & HISTORY

Fair Annie was first told by Marie de France in her *Lais of Marie de France* around 1180, though it is thought to be older. It did not appear in the Scottish record until the 18th century, and then most notably in Sir Walter Scott's *The Minstrelsy of the Scottish Border*.

SELECTED RECORDINGS

Peter Bellamy, *Fair Annie* (1974)

Frankie Armstrong, *Fair Annie* (1980)

Martin Simpson, *Fair Annie* (2001)

Susan McKeown, *Fair Annie* (2004)

Young Hunting

Child No. 68: A woman asks Young Hunting to stay the night with her. When he refuses, she gets him drunk, stabs him to death, and throws him in the river. The king then searches for Hunting and is told by a songbird of his murder, where he lies, and who killed him. The king finds the woman and has her burned at the stake for her crime.

68A.1 O lady, rock never your young son young
     One hour longer for me,
     For I have a sweetheart in Garlick's Wells
     I love thrice better than thee.

68A.2 'The very sols of my love's feet
     Is whiter then thy face:'
     'But nevertheless na, Young Hunting,
     Ye'l stay wi me all night.'

68A.3 She has birld in him Young Hunting
     The good ale and the beer,
     Till he was as fou drunken
     As any wild-wood steer.

68A.4 She has birld in him Young Hunting
     The good ale and the wine,
     Till he was as fou drunken
     As any wild-wood swine.

68A.5   Up she has tain him Young Hunting,
              And she has had him to her bed,
              * * * * *
              * * * * *

68A.6   And she has minded her on a little penknife,
              That hangs low down by her gare,
              And she has gin him Young Hunting
              A deep wound and a sare.

68A.7   Out an spake the bonny bird,
              That flew abon her head:
              'Lady, keep well thy green clothing
              Fra that good lord's blood.'

68A.8   'O better I'll keep my green clothing
              Fra that good lord's blood
              Nor thou can keep thy flattering toung,
              That flatters in thy head.

68A.9   'Light down, light down, my bonny bird,
              Light down upon my hand,
              * * * * *
              * * * * *

68A.10   'O siller, O siller shall be thy hire,
              An goud shall be thy fee,
              An every month into the year,
              Thy cage shall changed be.'

68A.11   'I winna light down, I shanna light down,
              I winna light on thy hand;

For soon, soon wad ye do to me
As ye done to Young Hunting.'

68A.12 She has booted an spird him Young Hunting
As he had been gan to ride,
A hunting-horn about his neck,
An the sharp sourd by his side.

68A.13 And she has had him to yon wan water,
For a' man calls it Clyde,
* * * * *
* * * * *

68A.14 The deepest pot intill it all
She has puten Young Hunting in;
A green truff upon his breast,
To hold that good lord down.

68A.15 It fell once upon a day
The king was going to ride,
And he sent for him Young Hunting,
To ride on his right side.

68A.16 She has turnd her right and round about,
She sware now by the corn,
'I saw na thy son, Young Hunting,
Sen yesterday at morn.'

68A.17 She has turnd her right and round about,
She swear now by the moon,
'I saw na thy son, Young Hunting,
Sen yesterday at noon.

68A.18 'It fears me sair in Clyde Water
That he is drownd therein:'
O thay ha sent for the king's duckers,
To duck for Young Hunting.

68A.19 They ducked in at the tae water-bank,
Thay ducked out at the tither:
'We'll duck no more for Young Hunting,
All tho he wear our brother.'

68A.20 Out an spake the bonny bird,
That flew abon their heads,
  * * * * *
  * * * * *

68A.21 'O he's na drownd in Clyde Water,
He is slain and put therein;
The lady that lives in yon castil
Slew him and put him in.

68A.22 'Leave aff your ducking on the day,
And duck upon the night;
Whear ever that sakeless knight lys slain,
The candels will shine bright.'

68A.23 Thay left off their ducking o the day,
And ducked upon the night,
And where that sakeless knight lay slain,
The candles shone full bright.

68A.24 The deepest pot intill it a'
Thay got Young Hunting in;

A green turff upon his brest,
To hold that good lord down.

68A.25 O thay ha sent aff men to the wood
To hew down baith thorn an fern,
That they might get a great bonefire
To burn that lady in.
'Put na the wyte on me,' she says,
'It was her May Catheren.'

68A.26 Whan thay had tane her May Catheren,
In the bonefire set her in;
It wad na take upon her cheeks,
Nor take upon her chin,
Nor yet upon her yallow hair,
To healle the deadly sin.

68A.27 Out they hae tain her May Catheren,
And they hay put that lady in;
O it took upon her cheek, her cheek,
An it took upon her chin,
An it took on her fair body,
She burnt like hoky-gren.

BALLAD NOTES & HISTORY

This ballad has its origin in 18th century Scotland and is known by many names, including *Earl Richard* or *The Proud Girl* in the United Kingdom, and *Henry Lee* or *Love Henry* in the United States. A recording by bluesman Dick Justice was collected by Harry Smith for his influential *Anthology of American Folk Music* in 1952, which helped to bolster the ballad's popularity with American artists.

SELECTED RECORDINGS

Dick Justice, *Henry Lee* (1929)

A.L. Lloyd, *The Proud Girl* (1972)

Bob Dylan, *Love Henry* (1993)

Nick Cave & the Bad Seeds, *Henry Lee* (1996)

Martin Simpson, *Love Henry* (2005)

Frankie Armstrong, *The Proud Girl (Child 68)* (2006)

Fair Margaret and Sweet William

Child No. 74: From her chamber window, Margaret watches the marriage procession of her lover William and another woman. That night her ghost appears before William, wishing him well but revealing she has died. The next morning William goes to find Margaret and is told by her brothers that she is indeed dead. He dies then of a broken heart and is buried near her in the church, where roses grow from their graves.

74A.1 As it fell out on a long summer's day,
   Two lovers they sat on a hill;
   They sat together that long summer's day,
   And could not talk their fill.

74A.2 'I see no harm by you, Margaret,
   Nor you see none by me;
   Before tomorrow eight a clock
   A rich wedding shall you see.'

74A.3 Fair Margaret sat in her bower-window,
   A combing of her hair,
   And there she spy'd Sweet William and his bride,
   As they were riding near.

74A.4 Down she layd her ivory comb,
    And up she bound her hair;
    She went her way forth of her bower,
    But never more did come there.

74A.5 When day was gone, and night was come,
    And all men fast asleep,
    Then came the spirit of Fair Margaret,
    And stood at William's feet.

74A.6 'God give you joy, you two true lovers,
    In bride-bed fast asleep;
    Loe I am going to my green grass grave,
    And am in my winding-sheet.'

74A.7 When day was come, and night was gone,
    And all men wak'd from sleep,
    Sweet William to his lady said,
    My dear, I have cause to weep.

74A.8 'I dreamd a dream, my dear lady;
    Such dreams are never good;
    I dreamd my bower was full of red swine,
    And my bride-bed full of blood.'

74A.9 'Such dreams, such dreams, my honoured lord,
    They never do prove good,
    To dream thy bower was full of swine,
    And [thy] bride-bed full of blood.'

74A.10 He called up his merry men all,
    By one, by two, and by three,

Saying, I'll away to Fair Margaret's bower,
By the leave of my lady.

74A.11 And when he came to Fair Margaret's bower,
He knocked at the ring;
So ready was her seven brethren
To let Sweet William in.

74A.12 He turned up the covering-sheet:
'Pray let me see the dead;
Methinks she does look pale and wan,
She has lost her cherry red.

74A.13 'I'll do more for thee, Margaret,
Than any of thy kin;
For I will kiss thy pale wan lips,
Tho a smile I cannot win.'

74A.14 With that bespeak her seven brethren,
Making most pitious moan:
'You may go kiss your jolly brown bride,
And let our sister alone.'

74A.15 'If I do kiss my jolly brown bride,
I do but what is right;
For I made no vow to your sister dear,
By day or yet by night.

74A.16 'Pray tell me then how much you'll deal
Of your white bread and your wine;
So much as is dealt at her funeral today
Tomorrow shall be dealt at mine.'

74A.17   Fair Margaret dy'd today, today,
          Sweet William he dy'd the morrow;
          Fair Margaret dy'd for pure true love,
          Sweet William he dy'd for sorrow.

74A.18   Margaret was buried in the lower chancel,
          Sweet William in the higher;
          Out of her breast there sprung a rose,
          And out of his a brier.

74A.19   They grew as high as the church-top,
          Till they could grow no higher,
          And then they grew in a true lovers' knot,
          Which made all people admire.

74A.20   There came the clerk of the parish,
          As you this truth shall hear,
          And by misfortune cut them down,
          Or they had now been there.

BALLAD NOTES & HISTORY

This ballad dates to as early as 1611, when it was included
in the play *The Knight of the Burning Pestle*. It has been part

of the American folk tradition since at least 1823. Regional variations are known by many titles such as *Pretty Polly and Sweet William, Fair Margaret's Misfortune, Sweet William's Bride,* and *False William.*

SELECTED RECORDINGS

A.L. Lloyd, *Fair Margaret and Sweet William* (1956)

Pete Seeger, *Fair Margaret* (1957)

Shirley Collins, *Lady Margaret and Sweet William* (1976)

Tim O'Brien, *Fair Margaret and Sweet William (Lady Margaret)* (1999)

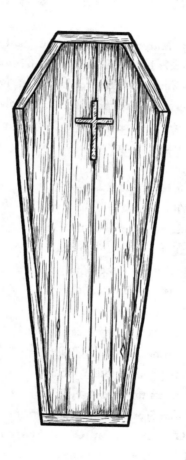

Sweet William's Ghost

Child No. 77: Margret is visited by the ghost of her lover, William, who asks her to release him from his vow to marry her. When she insists that he keep his pledge, he reveals that he cannot because he is dead. She then absolves him from his promise, travels the night to his burial place, and promptly dies upon his grave.

77A.1   There came a ghost to Margret's door,
With many a grievous groan,
And ay he tirled at the pin,
But answer made she none.

77A.2   'Is that my father Philip,
Or is't my brother John?
Or is't my true-love, Willy,
From Scotland new come home?'

77A.3   ''Tis not thy father Philip,
Nor yet thy brother John;
But 'tis thy true-love, Willy,
From Scotland new come home.

77A.4   'O sweet Margret, O dear Margret,
I pray thee speak to me;
Give me my faith and troth, Margret,
As I gave it to thee.'

77A.5 'Thy faith and troth thou's never get,
Nor yet will I thee lend,
Till that thou come within my bower,
And kiss my cheek and chin.'

77A.6 'If I shoud come within thy bower,
I am no earthly man;
And shoud I kiss thy rosy lips,
Thy days will not be lang.

77A.7 'O sweet Margret, O dear Margret,
I pray thee speak to me;
Give me my faith and troth, Margret,
As I gave it to thee.'

77A.8 'Thy faith and troth thou's never get,
Nor yet will I thee lend,
Till you take me to yon kirk,
And wed me with a ring.'

77A.9 'My bones are buried in yon kirk-yard,
Afar beyond the sea,
And it is but my spirit, Margret,
That's now speaking to thee.'

77A.10 She stretchd out her lilly-white hand,
And, for to do her best,
'Hae, there's your faith and troth, Willy,
God send your soul good rest.'

77A.11 Now she has kilted her robes of green
A piece below her knee,

And a' the live-lang winter night
The dead corp followed she.

77A.12   'Is there any room at your head, Willy?
Or any room at your feet?
Or any room at your side, Willy,
Wherein that I may creep?'

77A.13   'There's no room at my head, Margret,
There's no room at my feet;
There's no room at my side, Margret,
My coffin's made so meet.'

77A.14   Then up and crew the red, red cock,
And up then crew the gray:
'Tis time, tis time, my dear Margret,
That you were going away.'

77A.15   No more the ghost to Margret said,
But, with a grievous groan,
Evanishd in a cloud of mist,
And left her all alone.

77A.16   'O stay, my only true-love, stay,'
The constant Margret cry'd;
Wan grew her cheeks, she closd her een,
Stretchd her soft limbs, and dy'd.

BALLAD NOTES & HISTORY

This ballad dates to before 1740 and has many lyrical and musical variations. Sir Walter Scott based his poem *Advertisement to the Pirate* on the ballad, having been told the story by a woman in Shetland, Scotland.

SELECTED RECORDINGS

The Spinners, *Sweet William's Ghost* (1967)

Kate Rusby, *Sweet William's Ghost* (2003)

Cara, *Sweet William's Ghost* (2013)

The Unquiet Grave

Child No. 78: A maiden mourns the death of her true love, holding vigil over his grave for twelve months and a day. At last his ghost appears and she begs of him a kiss. He obliges, then informs her that she too now will soon be dead.

78B.1　　'How cold the wind do blow, dear love,
　　　　　And see the drops of rain!
　　　　　I never had but one true-love,
　　　　　In the green wood he was slain.

78B.2　　'I would do as much for my own true-love
　　　　　As in my power doth lay;
　　　　　I would sit and mourn all on his grave
　　　　　For a twelvemonth and a day.'

78B.3　　A twelvemonth and a day being past,
　　　　　His ghost did rise and speak:
　　　　　'What makes you mourn all on my grave?
　　　　　For you will not let me sleep.'

78B.4　　'It is not your gold I want, dear love,
　　　　　Nor yet your wealth I crave;
　　　　　But one kiss from your lily-white lips
　　　　　Is all I wish to have.

78B.5　　'Your lips are cold as clay, dear love,
　　　　　Your breath doth smell so strong;'

'I am afraid, my pretty, pretty maid,
Your time will not be long.'

BALLAD NOTES & HISTORY

Dating back to at least 1400, this ballad is close in theme and verse to *Sweet William's Ghost*. One of the more common tunes used for the ballad is the same used for the Irish pub song *Star of the County Down*.

SELECTED RECORDINGS

A.L. Lloyd, *The Unquiet Grave* (1956)

Shirley Collins, *The Unquiet Grave* (1959)

Joan Baez, *The Unquiet Grave* (1964)

Frankie Armstrong, *The Unquiet Grave* (1971)

The Dubliners, *The Unquiet Grave* (1975)

Kate Rusby, *The Unquiet Grave* (1999)

Papa M, *The Unquiet Grave* (2001)

The Wife of Usher's Well

Child No. 79: A woman sends her three sons across the sea, and weeks later learns that they have died. Her grief brings them back as ghosts to visit her for a night.

79A.1
There lived a wife at Usher's Well,
And a wealthy wife was she;
She had three stout and stalwart sons,
And sent them oer the sea.

79A.2
They hadna been a week from her,
A week but barely ane,
Whan word came to the carline wife
That her three sons were gane.

79A.3
They hadna been a week from her,
A week but barely three,
Whan word came to the carlin wife
That her sons she'd never see.

79A.4
'I wish the wind may never cease,
Nor fashes in the flood,
Till my three sons come hame to me,
In earthly flesh and blood.'

79A.5
It fell about the Martinmass,
When nights are lang and mirk,

The carlin wife's three sons came hame,
And their hats were o the birk.

79A.6   It neither grew in syke nor ditch,
Nor yet in ony sheugh;
But at the gates o Paradise,
That birk grew fair eneugh.
* * * * *

79A.7   'Blow up the fire, my maidens,
Bring water from the well;
For a' my house shall feast this night,
Since my three sons are well.'

79A.8   And she has made to them a bed,
She's made it large and wide,
And she's taen her mantle her about,
Sat down at the bed-side.
* * * * *

79A.9   Up then crew the red, red cock,
And up and crew the gray;
The eldest to the youngest said,
'Tis time we were away.

79A.10   The cock he hadna crawd but once,
And clappd his wings at a',
When the youngest to the eldest said,
Brother, we must awa.

79A.11   'The cock doth craw, the day doth daw,
The channerin worm doth chide;

Gin we be mist out o our place,
A sair pain we maun bide.

79A.12   'Fare ye weel, my mother dear!
Fareweel to barn and byre!
And fare ye weel, the bonny lass
Fareweel to barn and byre!
And fare ye weel, the bonny lass
That kindles my mother's fire!'

BALLAD NOTES & HISTORY

Dating to well before 1802, when it was first printed in Sir Walter Scott's *The Minstrelsy of the Scottish Border*, no complete version of this English ballad as it was originally written exists. By the 1890's it had become popular in North America's Appalachian region. In 2010, it served as the inspiration for a play by the same name about a mother whose son is killed in the war in Afghanistan.

SELECTED RECORDINGS

Peggy Seeger, *The Wife of Usher's Well* (1957)

Pete & Chris Coe, *The Wife of Usher's Well* (1972)

Steeleye Span, *The Wife of Usher's Well* (1975)

Frankie Armstrong, *The Wife of Usher's Well* (1996)

Martin Carthy, *The Wife of Usher's Well* (1998)

Alasdair Roberts, *The Wife of Usher's Well* (2001)

Martin Simpson, *Lady Gay* (2013)

Little Musgrave and Lady Barnard

Child No. 81: While at church, the rake Little Musgrave spies the beautiful wife of Lord Barnard and wins her over with his charm. Together they sneak away to her bower, but are betrayed by Lady Barnard's page. Lord Barnard finds them and kills Little Musgrave in a duel. After confessing her love for Musgrave, Lady Barnard is killed as well and the two are buried together in the same grave.

81A. It fell one holy-day,

  Refrain: Hay downe

 As many be in the yeare,

 When young men and maids together did goe,

 Their mattins and masse to heare,

81A.2 Little Musgrave came to the church-dore;

 The preist was at private masse;

 But he had more minde of the faire women

 Then he had of our lady['s] grace.

81A.3 The one of them was clad in green,

 Another was clad in pall,

 And then came in my Lord Barnard's wife,

 The fairest amonst them all.

81A.4 She cast an eye on Little Musgrave,
   As bright as the summer sun;
   And then bethought this Little Musgrave,
   This lady's heart have I woonn.

81A.5 Quoth she, I have loved thee, Little Musgrave,
   Full long and many a day;
   'So have I loved you, fair lady,
   Yet never word durst I say.'

81A.6 'I have a bower at Buckelsfordbery,
   Full daintyly it is deight;
   If thou wilt wend thither, thou Little Musgrave,
   Thou's lig in mine armes all night.'

81A.7 Quoth he, I thank yee, faire lady,
   This kindnes thou showest to me;
   But whether it be to my weal or woe,
   This night I will lig with thee.

81A.8 With that he heard, a little tyn page,
   By this ladye's coach as he ran:
   'All though I am my ladye's foot-page,
   Yet I am Lord Barnard's man.

81A.9 'My Lord Barnard shall knowe of this,
   Whether I sink or swim;'
   And ever where the bridges were broake
   He laid him downe to swimme.

81A.10 'A sleepe or wake, thou Lord Barnard,
   As thou art a man of life,

For Little Musgrave is at Bucklesfordbery,
A bed with thy own wedded wife.'

81A.11 'If this be true, thou little tinny page,
This thing thou tellest to me,
Then all the land in Bucklesfordbery
I freely will give to thee.

81A.12 'But if it be a ly, thou little tinny page,
This thing thou tellest to me,
On the hyest tree in Bucklesfordbery
Then hanged shalt thou be.'

81A.13 He called up his merry men all:
'Come saddle me my steed;
This night must I to Buckellsfordbery,
For I never had greater need.'

81A.14 And some of them whistld, and some
of them sung,
And some these words did say,
And ever when my Lord Barnard's horn blew,
'Away, Musgrave, away!'

81A.15 'Methinks I hear the thresel-cock,
Methinks I hear the jaye;
Methinks I hear my Lord Barnard,
And I would I were away.'

81A.16 'Lye still, lye still, thou Little Musgrave,
And huggell me from the cold;

'Tis nothing but a shephard's boy,
A driving his sheep to the fold.

81A.17   'Is not thy hawke upon a perch?
Thy steed eats oats and hay;
And thou a fair lady in thine armes,
And wouldst thou bee away?'

81A.18   With that my Lord Barnard came to the dore,
And lit a stone upon;
He plucked out three silver keys,
And he opend the dores each one.

81A.19   He lifted up the coverlett,
He lifted up the sheet:
'How now, how now, thou Littell Musgrave,
Doest thou find my lady sweet?'

81A.20   'I find her sweet,' quoth Little Musgrave,
'The more 'tis to my paine;
I would gladly give three hundred pounds
That I were on yonder plaine.'

81A.21   'Arise, arise, thou Littell Musgrave,
And put thy cloth s on;
It shall nere be said in my country
I have killed a naked man.

81A.22   'I have two swords in one scabberd,
Full deere they cost my purse;
And thou shalt have the best of them,
And I will have the worse.'

81A.23   The first stroke that Little Musgrave stroke,
       He hurt Lord Barnard sore;
       The next stroke that Lord Barnard stroke,
       Little Musgrave nere struck more.

81A.24   With that bespake this faire lady,
       In bed whereas she lay:
       'Although thou'rt dead, thou Little Musgrave,
       Yet I for thee will pray.

81A.25   'And wish well to thy soule will I,
       So long as I have life;
       So will I not for thee, Barnard,
       Although I am thy wedded wife.'

81A.26   He cut her paps from off her brest;
       Great pitty it was to see
       That some drops of this ladie's heart's blood
       Ran trickling downe her knee.

81A.27   'Woe worth you, woe worth, my mery men all
       You were nere borne for my good;
       Why did you not offer to stay my hand,
       When you see me wax so wood?

81A.28   'For I have slaine the bravest sir knight
       That ever rode on steed;
       So have I done the fairest lady
       That ever did woman's deed.

81A.29   'A grave, a grave,' Lord Barnard cryd,
       'To put these lovers in;

But lay my lady on the upper hand,
For she came of the better kin.'

BALLAD NOTES & HISTORY

The earliest printing of this ballad is thought to be a broadside dated to around 1641. The earliest known reference is from the play *The Knight of the Burning Pestle* in 1611. Over 300 versions of this ballad have been collected in Scotland, England, the United States, Canada and even the Caribbean Islands under such titles as *The Lamentable Ditty of the Little Mousgrove and the Lady Barnet*, *Lord Barnett and Little Munsgrove*, *Matty Grove*, *Matthy Groves*, and *Little Sir Grove* to name a few.

SELECTED RECORDINGS

Peggy Seeger & Ewan MacColl, *Matty Groves* (1961)

Joan Baez, *Matty Groves* (1962)

Fairport Convention, *Matty Groves* (1969)

Doc Watson, *Matty Groves* (1969)

Martin Carthy & Dave Swarbrick,
Little Musgrave and Lady Barnard (1969)

Nic Jones, *Little Musgrave* (1970)

Frankie Armstrong, *Little Musgrave* (1975)

Planxty, *Little Musgrave* (1980)

Ralph Stanley, *Little Mathie Grove* (2002)

Martin Simpson, *Little Musgrave* (2007)

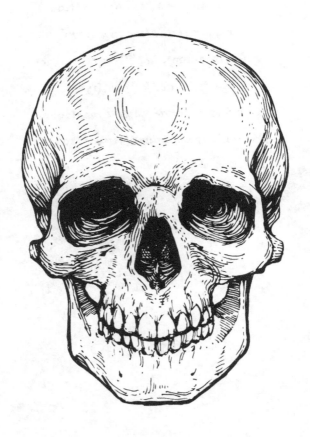

Bonny Barbara Allen

Child No. 84: A servant asks Barbara Allen to meet with his dying master. She agrees to go, but refuses all requests to tend to him. Soon after the man's death, Barbara Allen dies herself of a broken heart and is buried beside him.

84B.1 In Scarlet Town, where I was bound,
   There was a fair maid dwelling,
   Whom I had chosen to be my own,
   And her name it was Barbara Allen.

84B.2 All in the merry month of May,
   When green leaves they was springing,
   This young man on his death-bed lay,
   For the love of Barbara Allen.

84B.3 He sent his man unto her then,
   To the town where she was dwelling:
   'You must come to my master dear,
   If your name be Barbara Allen.

84B.4 'For death is printed in his face,
   And sorrow's in him dwelling,
   And you must come to my master dear,
   If your name be Barbara Allen.'

84B.5 'If death be printed in his face,
   And sorrow's in him dwelling,

Then little better shall he be
For bonny Barbara Allen.'

84B.6 So slowly, slowly she got up,
And so slowly she came to him,
And all she said when she came there,
Young man, I think you are a dying.

84B.7 He turnd his face unto her then:
'If you be Barbara Allen,
My dear,' said he, 'Come pitty me,
As on my death-bed I am lying.'

84B.8 'If on your death-bed you be lying,
What is that to Barbara Allen?
I cannot keep you from [your] death;
So farewell,' said Barbara Allen.

84B.9 He turnd his face unto the wall,
And death came creeping to him:
'Then adieu, adieu, and adieu to all,
And adieu to Barbara Allen!'

84B.10 And as she was walking on a day,
She heard the bell a ringing,
And it did seem to ring to her
'Unworthy Barbara Allen.'

84B.11 She turnd herself round about,
And she spy'd the corps a coming:
'Lay down, lay down the corps of clay,
That I may look upon him.'

84B.12 And all the while she looked on,
   So loudly she lay laughing,
   While all her friends cry'd [out] amain,
   'Unworthy Barbara Allen!'

84B.13 When he was dead, and laid in grave,
   Then death came creeping to she:
   'O mother, mother, make my bed,
   For his death hath quite undone me.

84B.14 'A hard-hearted creature that I was,
   To slight one that lovd me so dearly;
   I wish I had been more kinder to him,
   The time of his life when he was near me.'

84B.15 So this maid she then did die,
   And desired to be buried by him,
   And repented her self before she dy'd,
   That ever she did deny him.

BALLAD NOTES & HISTORY

Dating to before 1666, *Bonny Barbara Allen* is considered by many to be the most widely collected song in the English language, with versions popular in England, Scotland, and the United States. The ballad is known by many names, including *The Ballet of Barbara Allen*, *Barbara Allen's Cruelty*, *Barbarous Ellen*, *Edelin*, *Hard Hearted Barbary Ellen*, *The Sad Ballad of Little Johnnie Green*, *Sir John Graham*, and *Barbry Allen*, among others. A British broadside from 1690 used the title *Barbara Allen's cruelty: or, the young-man's tragedy. With Barbara Allen's [l]amentation for her unkindness to her lover, and her self.*

SELECTED RECORDINGS

Ewan MacColl, *Bawbee Allen* (1956)

The Everly Brothers, *Barbara Allen* (1958)

Shirley Collins, *Barbara Allen* (1959)

Jean Ritchie, *Barbry Allen* (1961)

Joan Baez, *Barbara Allen* (1961)

Simon & Garfunkel, *Barbriallen* (1964)

Jerry Reed, *Barbara Allen* (1973)

Bob Dylan, *Barbara Allen* (1989)

Dolly Parton, *Barbara Allen* (1994)

Martin Carthy, *Barbary Ellen* (1998)

Frankie Armstrong, *Barbara Allen* (2000)

FAVORITE ENGLISH & SCOTTISH BALLADS

John Travolta, *Barbara Allen* (2005)

Colin Meloy, *Barbara Allen* (2008)

Alasdair Roberts, *Barbara Allen* (2010)

Norah Jones & Billie Joe Armstrong, *Barbara Allen* (2013)

Fause Foodrage

Child No. 89: A group of nobles, Fa'se Footrage among them, rebels against the king. Footrage sneaks into the royal castle and finds the king and queen in bed. The king he kills, but the queen pleads for him to spare her until her babe is born. He agrees but tells her if the babe is a boy, he will see it hanged. Footrage imprisons the queen, but she escapes and has her child—a boy—in a pigsty. A man named Wise William sends his wife to find her and when she does, the queen convinces the wife to exchange William's daughter for her newborn son to save him from the gallows. The wife agrees and when the boy is grown and the truth of his lineage revealed, he kills Footrage in revenge, then marries the daughter the queen has raised as her own.

89A.1 King Eaterhas courted her for her gowd,
     King Wester for her fee,
     King Honor for her lands sae braid,
     And for her fair body.

89A.2 They had not been four months married,
     As I have heard them tell,
     Until the nobles of the land
     Against them did rebel.

89A.3 And they cast kaivles them amang,
   And kaivles them between,
   And they cast kaivles them amang
   Wha shoud gae kill the king.

89A.4 O some said yea, and some said nay,
   Their words did not agree;
   Till up it gat him Fa'se Footrage,
   And sware it shoud be he.

89A.5 When bells were rung, and mass was sung,
   And a' man boon to bed,
   King Honor and his gay ladie
   In a hie chamer were laid.

89A.6 Then up it raise him Fa'se Footrage,
   While a' were fast asleep,
   And slew the porter in his lodge,
   That watch and ward did keep.

89A.7 O four and twenty silver keys
   Hang hie upon a pin,
   And ay as a door he did unlock,
   He has fastend it him behind.

89A.8 Then up it raise him King Honor,
   Says, What means a' this din!
   Now what's the matter, Fa'se Footrage?
   O wha was't loot you in?

89A.9   'O ye my errand well shall learn
Before that I depart;'
Then drew a knife baith lang and sharp
And pierced him thro the heart.

89A.10   Then up it got the Queen hersell,
And fell low down on her knee:
'O spare my life now, Fa'se Footrage!
For I never injured thee.

89A.11   'O spare my life now, Fa'se Footrage!
Until I lighter be,
And see gin it be lad or lass
King Honor has left me wi.'

89A.12   'O gin it be a lass,' he says,
'Well nursed she shall be;
But gin it be a lad-bairn,
He shall be hanged hie.

89A.13   'I winna spare his tender age,
Nor yet his hie, hie kin;
But as soon as eer he born is,
He shall mount the gallows-pin.'

89A.14   O four and twenty valiant knights
Were set the Queen to guard,
And four stood ay at her bower-door,
To keep baith watch and ward.

89A.15   But when the time drew till an end
That she should lighter be,

She cast about to find a wile
To set her body free.

89A.16   O she has birled these merry young men
Wi strong beer and wi wine,
Until she made them a' as drunk
As any wallwood swine.

89A.17   'O narrow, narrow is this window,
And big, big am I grown!'
Yet thro the might of Our Ladie
Out at it she has won.

89A.18   She wanderd up, she wanderd down,
She wanderd out and in,
And at last, into the very swines' stye,
The Queen brought forth a son.

89A.19   Then they cast kaivles them amang
Wha should gae seek the Queen,
And the kaivle fell upon Wise William,
And he's sent his wife for him.

89A.20   O when she saw Wise William's wife,
The Queen fell on her knee;
'Win up, win up, madame,' she says,
'What means this courtesie?'

89A.21   'O out of this I winna rise
Till a boon ye grant to me,
To change your lass for this lad-bairn
King Honor left me wi.

89A.22   'And ye maun learn my gay gose-hawke
        Well how to breast a steed,
        And I shall learn your turtle-dow
        As well to write and read.

89A.23   'And ye maun learn my gay gose-hawke
        To wield baith bow and brand,
        And I shall learn your turtle-dow
        To lay gowd wi her hand.

89A.24   'At kirk or market where we meet,
        We dare nae mair avow
        But, Dame how does my gay gose-hawk?
        Madame, how does my dow?'

89A.25   When days were gane, and years came on,
        Wise William he thought long;
        Out has he taen King Honor's son,
        A hunting for to gang.

89A.26   It sae fell out at their hunting,
        Upon a summer's day,
        That they cam by a fair castle,
        Stood on a sunny brae.

89A.27   'O dinna ye see that bonny castle,
        Wi wa's and towers sae fair?
        Gin ilka man had back his ain,
        Of it you shoud be heir.'

89A.28   'How I shoud be heir of that castle
        In sooth I canna see,

When it belongs to Fa'se Footrage,
And he's nae kin to me.'

89A.29 'O gin ye shoud kill him Fa'se Footrage,
You woud do what is right;
For I wot he killd your father dear,
Ere ever you saw the light.

89A.30 'Gin you should kill him Fa'se Footrage,
There is nae man durst you blame;
For he keeps your mother a prisoner,
And she dares no take you hame.'

89A.31 The boy stared wild like a gray gose-hawke,
Says, What may a' this mean!
'My boy, you are King Honor's son,
And your mother's our lawful queen.'

89A.32 'O gin I be King Honor's son,
By Our Ladie I swear,
This day I will that traytour slay,
And relieve my mother dear.'

89A.33 He has sent his bent bow till his breast,
And lap the castle-wa,
And soon he's siesed on Fa'se Footrage,
Wha loud for help gan ca.

89A.34 'O hold your tongue now, Fa'se Footrage,
Frae me you shanno flee;'
Syne pierced him through the foul fa'se heart,
And set his mother free.

89A.35   And he has rewarded Wise William
           Wi the best half of his land,
           And sae has he the turtle-dow
           Wi the truth of his right hand.

BALLAD NOTES & HISTORY

This ballad dates back to at least the mid 1700's. Child collected a version named *The East Muir King* from Amelia and Jane Harris, sisters well known for their vast repertoire. *Willie O Winsbury*, Child No. 100, is often mistakenly sung to its tune.

SELECTED RECORDINGS

Hermes Nye, *King O'Love/Fause Foodrage* (1957)

Brian Peters, *Fause Foodrage* (1992)

Chris Coe, *Fause Foodrage* (2001)

Kathrine Campbell, *East Muir King* (2004)

Lamkin

Child No. 93: The mason Lamkin builds a castle for his lord, who refuses to pay him for his work. While the lord is away, Lamkin sneaks into the castle and kills the lord's wife and infant son in revenge. Upon returning home, the lord finds his castle is red with the blood of his murdered family.

93A.1   It's Lamkin was a mason good
    As ever built wi stane;
    He built Lord Wearie's castle,
    But payment got he nane.

93A.2   'O pay me, Lord Wearie,
    come, pay me my fee:'
    'I canna pay you, Lamkin,
    For I maun gang oer the sea.'

93A.3   'O pay me now, Lord Wearie,
    Come, pay me out o hand:'
    'I canna pay you, Lamkin,
    Unless I sell my land.'

93A.4   'O gin ye winna pay me,
    I here sall mak a vow,
    Before that ye come hame again,
    ye sall hae cause to rue.'

93A.5 Lord Wearie got a bonny ship,
  to sail the saut sea faem;
  Bade his lady weel the castle keep,
  ay till he should come hame.

93A.6 But the nourice was a fause limmer
  as eer hung on a tree;
  She laid a plot wi Lamkin,
  whan her lord was oer the sea.

93A.7 She laid a plot wi Lamkin,
  when the servants were awa,
  Loot him in at a little shot-window,
  and brought him to the ha.

93A.8 'O whare's a' the men o this house,
  that ca me Lamkin?'
  'They're at the barn-well thrashing;
  'twill be lang ere they come in.'

93A.9 'And whare's the women o this house,
  that ca me Lamkin?'
  'They're at the far well washing;
  'twill be lang ere they come in.'

93A.10 'And whare's the bairns o this house,
  that ca me Lamkin?'
  'They're at the school reading;
  'twill be night or they come hame.'

93A.11 'O whare's the lady o this house,
  that ca's me Lamkin?'

'She's up in her bower sewing,
but we soon can bring her down.'

93A.12   Then Lamkin's tane a sharp knife,
that hang down by his gaire,
And he has gien the bonny babe
A deep wound and a sair.

93A.13   Then Lamkin he rocked,
and the fause nourice sang,
Till frae ilkae bore o the cradle
the red blood out sprang.

93A.14   Then out it spak the lady,
as she stood on the stair:
'What ails my bairn, nourice,
that he's greeting sae sair?

93A.15   'O still my bairn, nourice,
O still him wi the pap!'
'He winna still, lady,
for this nor for that.'

93A.16   'O still my bairn, nourice,
O still him wi the wand!'
'He winna still, lady,
for a' his father's land.'

93A.17   'O still my bairn, nourice,
O still him wi the bell!'
'He winna still, lady,
till ye come down yoursel.'

93A.18 O the firsten step she steppit,
    she steppit on a stane;
    But the neisten step she steppit,
    she met him Lamkin.

93A.19 'O mercy, mercy, Lamkin,
    hae mercy upon me!
    Though you've taen my young son's life,
    Ye may let mysel be.'

93A.20 'O sall I kill her, nourice,
    or sall I lat her be?'
    'O kill her, kill her, Lamkin,
    for she neer was good to me.'

93A.21 'O scour the bason, nourice,
    and mak it fair and clean,
    For to keep this lady's heart's blood,
    For she's come o noble kin.'

93A.22 'There need nae bason, Lamkin,
    lat it run through the floor;
    What better is the heart's blood
    o the rich than o the poor?'

93A.23 But ere three months were at an end,
    Lord Wearie came again;
    But dowie, dowie was his heart
    when first he came hame.

93A.24 'O wha's blood is this,' he says,
    'That lies in the chamer?'

'It is your lady's heart's blood;
'tis as clear as the lamer.'

93A.25   'And wha's blood is this,' he says,
'That lies in my ha?'
'It is your young son's heart's blood;
'tis the clearest ava.'

93A.26   O sweetly sang the black-bird
that sat upon the tree;
But sairer grat Lamkin,
when he was condemnd to die.

93A.27   And bonny sang the mavis,
Out o the thorny brake;
But sairer grat the nourice,
when she was tied to the stake.

BALLAD NOTES & HISTORY

This ballad is popular in England, Scotland and the United States. While the story usually follows the same basic story, the mason goes by many names, including Long

Lonkin, Balankin, Lambert Linkin, Rankin, Long Lankyn, and Lammikin.

SELECTED RECORDINGS

A.L. Lloyd, *Long Lankin* (1956)

Martin Carthy, *Long Lankin* (1968)

Martin Simpson, *Beaulampkin* (1976)

Brian Peters, *Lamkin* (1985)

Alasdair Roberts, *Long Lankin* (2010)

Shirley Collins, *Cruel Lincoln* (2016)

The Maid Freed from the Gallows

Child No. 95: When a woman is sentenced to hang, various members of her family refuse to pay a bribe to save her from the gallows. At last her true love arrives and offers gold to her hangman to free her.

95A.1   * * * * *
'O good Lord Judge, and sweet Lord Judge,
Peace for a little while!
Methinks I see my own father,
Come riding by the stile.

95A.2   'Oh father, oh father, a little of your gold,
And likewise of your fee!
To keep my body from yonder grave,
And my neck from the gallows-tree.'

95A.3   'None of my gold now you shall have,
Nor likewise of my fee;
For I am come to see you hangd,
And hanged you shall be.'

95A.4   'Oh good Lord Judge, and sweet Lord Judge,
Peace for a little while!
Methinks I see my own mother,
Come riding by the stile.

95A.5   'Oh mother, oh mother, a little of your gold,
          And likewise of your fee,
          To keep my body from yonder grave,
          And my neck from the gallows-tree!'

95A.6   'None of my gold now shall you have,
          Nor likewise of my fee;
          For I am come to see you hangd,
          And hanged you shall be.'

95A.7   'Oh good Lord Judge, and sweet Lord Judge,
          Peace for a little while!
          Methinks I see my own brother,
          Come riding by the stile.

95A.8   'Oh brother, oh brother, a little of your gold,
          And likewise of your fee,
          To keep my body from yonder grave,
          And my neck from the gallows-tree!'

95A.9   'None of my gold now shall you have,
          Nor likewise of my fee;
          For I am come to see you hangd,
          And hanged you shall be.'

95A.10   'Oh good Lord Judge, and sweet Lord Judge,
          Peace for a little while!
          Methinks I see my own sister,
          Come riding by the stile.

95A.11 'Oh sister, oh sister, a little of your gold,
    And likewise of your fee,
    To keep my body from yonder grave,
    And my neck from the gallows-tree!'

95A.12 'None of my gold now shall you have,
    Nor likewise of my fee;
    For I am come to see you hangd,
    And hanged you shall be.'

95A.13 'Oh good Lord Judge, and sweet Lord Judge,
    Peace for a little while!
    Methinks I see my own true-love,
    Come riding by the stile.

95A.14 'Oh true-love, oh true-love, a little of your gold,
    And likewise of your fee,
    To save my body from yonder grave,
    And my neck from the gallows-tree.'

95A.15 'Some of my gold now you shall have,
    And likewise of my fee,
    For I am come to see you saved,
    And saved you shall be.'

BALLAD NOTES & HISTORY

Dating to before 1770, this ballad is widespread across Europe and the United States under many different names. There are dozens of variants in Finland alone. It was perhaps most famously recorded by Led Zeppelin as *Gallows Pole* on their 1970 album *Led Zeppelin III*. Bob Dylan used the basic story as the inspiration for his song *Seven Curses*, in which a daughter attempts to save her father from the hangman.

SELECTED RECORDINGS

Lead Belly, *The Gallis Pole* (1939)

John Jacob Niles, *The Maid Freed from the Gallows Pole* (1940)

Jean Ritchie, *The Hangman* (1957)

Odetta, *Gallows Pole* (1957)

Jimmy Driftwood, *Slack Your Rope* (1959)

The Kingston Trio, *Hangman* (1961)

Fred Gerlach, *Gallows Pole* (1962)

Tex Ritter, *Gallows Pole* (1965)

Led Zeppelin, *Gallows Pole* (1970)

Judy Collins, *Anathea* (1974)

Nic Jones, *Prickly Bush* (2002)

Neil Young & Crazy Horse, *Gallows Pole* (2012)

Willie O Winsbury

Child No. 100: Willie of Winsbury is sentenced to death for cavorting with the king's daughter. But upon seeing Willie, the king is so moved by the young man's handsome looks that he rescinds the sentence and instead offers his daughter to him in marriage.

100A.1 The king he hath been a prisoner,
   A prisoner lang in Spain,
   And Willie o the Winsbury
   Has lain lang wi his daughter at hame.

100A.2 'What aileth thee, my daughter Janet,
   Ye look so pale and wan?
   Have ye had any sore sickness,
   Or have ye been lying wi a man?
   Or is it for me, your father dear,
   And biding sae lang in Spain?'

100A.3 'I have not had any sore sickness,
   Nor yet been lying wi a man;
   But it is for you, my father dear,
   In biding sae lang in Spain.'

100A.4 'Cast ye off your berry-brown gown,
   Stand straight upon the stone,

That I may ken ye by yere shape,
Whether ye be a maiden or none.'

100A.5 She's coosten off her berry-brown gown,
Stooden straight upo yon stone;
Her apron was short, and her haunches
 were round,
Her face it was pale and wan.

100A.6 'Is it to a man o might, Janet?
Or is it to a man of fame?
Or is it to any of the rank robbers
That's lately come out o Spain?'

100A.7 'It is not to a man of might,' she said,
'Nor is it to a man of fame;
But it is to William of Winsbury;
I could lye nae langer my lane.'

100A.8 The king's called on his merry men all,
By thirty and by three:
'Go fetch me William of Winsbury,
For hanged he shall be.'

100A.9 But when he cam the king before,
He was clad o the red silk;
His hair was like to threeds o gold.
And his skin was as white as milk.

100A.10 'It is nae wonder,' said the king,
'That my daughter's love ye did win;

Had I been a woman, as I am a man,
My bedfellow ye should hae been.

100C.11 'O will you marry my daughter dear,
By the faith of thy right hand?
And thou shalt reign, when I am dead,
The king over my whole land.'

100C.12 'I will marry your daughter dear,
With my heart, yea and my hand;
But it never shall be that Lord Winsbury
Shall rule oer fair Scotland.'

100C.13 He's mounted her on a milk-white steed,
Himself on a dapple-grey,
And made her a lady of as much land
She could ride in a whole summer day.

BALLAD NOTES & HISTORY

This Scottish ballad dates back to at least 1775 and is known by many names, including *Lord Thomas of Winesberry* and *Johnnie Barbour*. It is often sung to the tune of Child No. 89, *Fause Foodrage*, rather than its own traditional tune.

SELECTED RECORDINGS

Sweeney's Men, *Willie O'Winsbury* (1968)

Anne Briggs, *Willie O Winsbury* (1971)

Pentangle, *Willie O'Winsbury* (1972)

Dick Gaughan, *Willie O'Winsbury* (1978)

Nic Jones, *William of Winesbury* (2002)

Richard Thompson, *Willie O'Winsbury* (2006)

Kate Rusby, *John Barbury* (2007)

Offa Rex, *Willie O'Winsbury* (2017)

Prince Heathen

Child No. 104: Margery May is raped by Prince Heathen and imprisoned until she bears his child. She begs of her captor some water to drink, but he refuses. Once the baby is born, she asks for a shred of silk in which to wrap it. Prince Heathen, his heart now softened, agrees to her request then declares his love for her.

104A.1 Lady Margery May sits in her bower,
    Sewing at her seem;
    By there comes a heathen knight,
    From her her maidenhead has tane.

104A.2 He has put her in a tower strong,
    With double locks on fifty doors:
    'Lady Margery May, will you ga now?'
    'O ye heathen knight, not yet for you.

104A.3 'I am asking, you heathen knight;
    What I am asking will you grant to me?
    Will ye let one of your waitmen
    A drink of your well bring to me?'

104A.4 'Meat nor drink you shall never get,
    Nor out of that shall you never come,
    Meat nor drink shall you never get,
    Until you bear to me daughter or son.'

104A.5   Thus time drew on, and further on,
         For travail came this young lady to;
         She travailed up, so did she down,
         But lighter could she never be.

104A.6   'An asking, an asking, you heathen knight;
         An asking will you grant to me?
         Will you give me a scread of silk,
         For to row your young son wi?'

104A.7   He took the horse-sheet in his hand,
         The tears came twinkling down:
         'Lady Margaret May, will ye ga now?'
         'O ye heathen knight, not yet for you.'

104A.8   'I'll wash my young son with the milk,
         I will dry my young son with the silk;
         For hearts will break, and bands will bow;
         So dear will I love my lady now!'

BALLAD NOTES & HISTORY

Little is known about this ballad's origin. Child's A version was taken from an undated text called *The*

Disconsolate Lady. It is very similar in story and theme to Child No. 5, *Gil Brenton.*

SELECTED RECORDINGS

Martin Carthy & Dave Swarbrick, *Prince Heathen* (1969)

A.L. Lloyd, *Prince Heathen* (1972)

Frankie Armstrong, *Prince Heathen* (1973)

Sylvia Barnes, *Prince Heathen* (2007)

The Furrow Collective, *Prince Heathen* (2016)

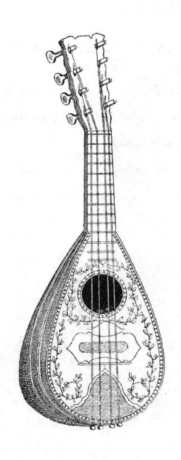

The Famous Flower of Serving Men

Child No. 106: A fair lady's husband is murdered by thieves. Fearing for her life, she cuts her hair and flees the castle disguised as a servant named Sweet William. She is taken into the king's service and becomes his trusted chamberlain. While the king is away hunting, the woman-turned-serving-man laments her fate and is overheard by an old man, who tells her story to the king upon his return. To everyone's surprise, the king then marries her.

106.1　　You beautious ladies, great and small,
　　　　　I write unto you one and all,
　　　　　Whereby that you may understand
　　　　　What I have suffered in this land.

106.2　　I was by birth a lady fair,
　　　　　My father's chief and onely heir,
　　　　　But when my good old father dy'd,
　　　　　Then was I made a young knight's bride.

106.3　　And then my love built me a bower,
　　　　　Bedeckt with many a fragrant flower;
　　　　　A braver bower you never did see
　　　　　Then my true-love did build for me.

106.4 But there came thieves late in the night,
They rob'd my bower, and slew my knight,
And after that my knight was slain,
I could no longer there remain.

106.5 My servants all from me did flye,
In the midst of my extremity,
And left me by my self alone,
With a heart more cold then any stone.

106.6 Yet, though my heart was full of care,
Heaven would not suffer me to despair;
Wherefore in hast I chang'd my name
From Fair Elise to Sweet William.

106.7 And therewithal I cut my hair,
And drest my self in man's attire,
My doublet, hose, and bever-hat,
And a golden band about my neck.

106.8 With a silver rapier by my side,
So like a gallant I did ride;
The thing that I delighted on,
Was for to be a serving-man.

106.9 Thus in my sumptuous man's array,
I bravely rode along the way;
And at the last it chanced so
That I unto the king's court did go.

106.10 Then to the king I bowed full low,
My love and duty for to show,

And so much favour I did crave
That I a serving-man's place might have.

106.11   'Stand up, brave youth, the king replyd,
'Thy service shall not be denyd;
But tell me first what thou canst do;
Thou shalt be fitted thereunto.

106.12   'Wilt thou be usher of my hall,
To wait upon my nobles all?
Or wilt thou be taster of my wine,
To wait on me when I shall dine?

106.13   'Or wilt thou be my chamberlain,
To make my bed both soft and fine?
Or wilt thou be one of my guard?
And I will give thee thy reward.'

106.14   Sweet William, with a smiling face,
Said to the king, If't please your grace
To show such favour unto me,
Your chamberlain I fain would be.

106.15   The king then did the nobles call,
To ask the counsel of them all,
Who gave consent Sweet William he
The king's own chamberlain should be.

106.16   Now mark what strange things come to pass:
As the king one day a hunting was,
With all his lords and noble train,
Sweet William did at home remain.

106.17   Sweet William had no company then
         With him at home but an old man;
         And when he saw the coast was clear,
         He took a lute which he had there.

106.18   Upon the lute Sweet William plaid,
         And to the same he sung and said,
         With a pleasant and most noble voice,
         Which made the old man to rejoyce:

106.19   'My father was as brave a lord
         As ever Europe did afford;
         My mother was a lady bright,
         My husband was a valiant knight.

106.20   'And I my self a lady gay,
         Bedeckt with gorgious rich array;
         The bravest lady in the land
         Had not more pleasures to command.

106.21   'I had my musick every day,
         Harmonious lessons for to play;
         I had my virgins fair and free,
         Continually to wait on me.

106.22   'But now, alas! my husband's dead,
         And all my friends are from me fled;
         My former joys are past and gone,
         For now I am a serving-man.'

106.23   At last the king from hunting came,
         And presently upon the same

He called for the good old man,
And thus to speak the king began.

106.24 'What news, what news, old man?' quod he;
'What news hast thou to tell to me?'
'Brave news,' the old man he did say;
'Sweet William is a lady gay.'

106.25 'If this be true thou tellest me
I'le make thee a lord of high degree;
But if thy words do prove a lye,
Thou shalt be hanged up presently.'

106.26 But when the king the truth had found,
His joys did more and more abound;
According as the old man did say,
Sweet William was a lady gay.

106.27 Therefore the king without delay
Put on her glorious rich array,
And upon her head a crown of gold,
Which was most famous to behold.

106.28 And then, for fear of further strife,
He took Sweet William for his wife;
The like before was never seen,
A serving-man to be a queen.

BALLAD NOTES & HISTORY

Unlike most of the ballads collected by Child, the authorship of *The Famous Flower of Serving Men* is well known. It was first published by famous balladeer Laurence Price in 1656 under the title *The famous Flower of Serving-Men. Or, The Lady turn'd Serving-Man.*

SELECTED RECORDINGS

Martin Carthy,
The Famous Flower of Serving Men (1972)

The Demon Barbers,
The Famous Flower of Serving Men (2005)

Sir Hugh or
The Jew's Daughter

Child No. 155: A boy, Sir Hugh, accidentally kicks his ball into the window of a castle. When he goes to fetch it, he is lured inside by a girl who lives there with her father. She then murders the boy and throws his body in a well. From beyond the grave, Sir Hugh tells his mother where to find his corpse so that he may be buried proper.

155A.1   Four and twenty bonny boys
       Were playing at the ba,

       And by it came him sweet Sir Hugh,

       And he playd oer them a'.

155A.2   He kickd the ba with his right foot,

       And catchd it wi his knee,

       And throuch-and-thro the Jew's window

       He gard the bonny ba flee.

155A.3   He's doen him to the Jew's castell,

       And walkd it round about;

       And there he saw the Jew's daughter,

       At the window looking out.

155A.4   'Throw down the ba, ye Jew's daughter,

       Throw down the ba to me!'

'Never a bit,' says the jew's daughter,
'Till up to me come ye.'

155A.5 'How will I come up? How can I come up?
How can I come to thee?
For as ye did to my auld father,
The same ye'll do to me.'

155A.6 She's gane to her father's garden,
And pu'd an apple red and green;
'Twas a' to wyle him sweet Sir Hugh,
And to entice him in.

155A.7 She's led him in through ae dark door,
And sae has she thro nine;
She's laid him on a dressing-table,
And stickit him like a swine.

155A.8 And first came out the thick, thick blood,
And syne came out the thin,
And syne came out the bonny heart's blood;
There was nae mair within.

155A.9 She's rowd him in a cake o lead,
Bade him lie still and sleep;
She's thrown him in Our Lady's draw-well,
Was fifty fathom deep.

155A.10 When bells were rung, and mass was sung,
And a' the bairns came hame,
When every lady gat hame her son,
The Lady Maisry gat nane.

155A.11   She's taen her mantle her about,
            Her coffer by the hand,
            And she's gane out to seek her son,
            And wanderd oer the land.

155A.12   She's doen her to the Jew's castell,
            Where a' were fast asleep:
            'Gin ye be there, my sweet Sir Hugh,
            I pray you to me speak.'

155A.13   She's doen her to the Jew's garden,
            Thought he had been gathering fruit:
            'Gin ye be there, my sweet Sir Hugh,
            I pray you to me speak.'

155A.14   She neard Our Lady's deep draw-well,
            Was fifty fathom deep:
            'Whareer ye be, my sweet Sir Hugh,
            I pray you to me speak.'

155A.15   'Gae hame, gae hame, my mither dear,
            Prepare my winding-sheet,
            And at the back o merry Lincoln
            The morn I will you meet.'

155A.16   Now Lady Maisry is gane hame,
            Made him a winding sheet,
            And at the back o merry Lincoln
            The dead corpse did her meet.

155A.17   And a' the bells of merry Lincoln
            Without men's hands were rung,

And a' the books o merry Lincoln
Were read without man's tongue,
And neer was such a burial
Sin Adam's days begun.

BALLAD NOTES & HISTORY

Dating to the late 1200's, *Sir Hugh* is one of the oldest ballads collected by Child. It is popular in England, Scotland, Canada, and the United States, where it's most often called *The Fatal Flower Garden*. It is based on the true story of Little Saint Hugh of Lincoln, whose accidental death was falsely blamed on Jews, resulting in 70 arrests and 18 hangings. Due to its reputation as an anti-Semitic blood libel, much has been written about the ballad, including the 1849 text by Abraham Hume entitled *Sir Hugh of Lincoln, or, an Examination of a Curious Tradition respecting the Jews, with a notice of the Popular Poetry connected with it.*

SELECTED RECORDINGS

Nelstone's Hawaiians, *Fatal Flower Garden* (1929)

A.L. Lloyd, *Sir Hugh* (1956)

The Ian Campbell Folk Group, *Little Sir Hugh* (1968)

Pete & Chris Coe, *Hugh of Lincoln* (1972)

Andrew Bird, *Fatal Flower Garden* (2001)

Peggy Seeger, *Fatal Flower Garden* (2003)

Alasdair Roberts, *Little Sir Hugh* (2010)

Sam Lee, *The Jew's Garden* (2012)

Geordie

Child No. 209: Geordie is arrested for killing a noble in battle. When Geordie's lady learns of his fate, she races to his execution to beg his pardon from the king. The king at first refuses, but is conviced by one of his lords to take a five-thousand-pound payment instead. The lady gladly pays with money collected from generous onlookers and Geordie is freed.

209A.1   There was a battle in the north,
And nobles there was many,
And they hae killd Sir Charlie Hay,
And they laid the wyte on Geordie.

209A.2   O he has written a lang letter,
He sent it to his lady:
'Ye maun cum up to Enbrugh town,
To see what word's o Geordie.'

209A.3   When first she lookd the letter on,
She was baith red and rosy;
But she had na read a word but twa
Till she wallowt like a lily.

209A.4   'Gar get to me my gude grey steed,
My menyie a' gae wi me,

For I shall neither eat nor drink
Till Enbrugh town shall see me.'

209A.5 And she has mountit her gude grey steed,
Her menyie a' gaed wi her,
And she did neither eat nor drink
Till Enbrugh town did see her.

209A.6 And first appeard the fatal block,
And syne the aix to head him,
And Geordie cumin down the stair,
And bands o airn upon him.

209A.7 But tho he was chaind in fetters strang,
O airn and steel sae heavy,
There was na ane in a' the court
Sae bra a man as Geordie.

209A.8 O she's down on her bended knee,
I wat she's pale and weary:
'O pardon, pardon, noble king,
And gie me back my dearie!

209A.9 'I hae born seven sons to my Geordie dear,
The seventh neer saw his daddie;
O pardon, pardon, noble king,
Pity a waefu lady!'

209A.10 'Gar bid the headin-man mak haste,'
Our king reply'd fu lordly:
'O noble king, tak a' that's mine,
But gie me back my Geordie!'

209A.11 The Gordons cam, and the Gordons ran,
   And they were stark and steady,
   And ay the word amang them a'
   Was, Gordons, keep you ready!

209A.12 An aged lord at the king's right hand
   Says, Noble king, but hear me;
   Gar her tell down five thousand pound,
   And gie her back her dearie.

209A.13 Some gae her marks, some gae her crowns,
   Some gae her dollars many,
   And she's telld down five thousand pound,
   And she's gotten again her dearie.

209A.14 She blinkit blythe in her Geordie's face,
   Says, Dear I've bought thee, Geordie;
   But there sud been bluidy bouks on the green
   Or I had tint my laddie.

209A.15 He claspit her by the middle sma,
   And he kist her lips sae rosy:
   'The fairest flower o woman-kind
   Is my sweet, bonie lady!'

BALLAD NOTES & HISTORY

Versions of this ballad have been found in Scotland, England, Ireland, Canada and the United States. The earliest known publication is an English broadside printed between 1672 and 1696 entitled *The Life and Death of George of Oxford*. In English variants, the lady usually comes too late and Geordie is executed.

SELECTED RECORDINGS

A.L. Lloyd, *Georgie* (1956)

Shirley Collins, *Geordie* (1959)

Ewan MacColl, *Geordie* (1960)

Joan Baez, *Geordie* (1967)

Doc Watson, *Georgie* (1967)

Peter Bellamy, *Geordie* (1968)

Martin Carthy, *Geordie* (1974)

Martin Simpson, *Georgie* (2003)

Anaïs Mitchell & Jefferson Hamer, *Geordie* (2013)

The Mother's Malison
or Clyde's Water

Child No. 216: Against the advice of his mother, Willie leaves to visit his lover, May Margaret, across the raging River Clyde. When he arrives he is turned away by her mother, then drowns on his return home. When May Margaret hears he had come to see her, she sets out to find him, and sadly shares his fate, also drowning in the Clyde.

216A.1 'Ye gie corn unto my horse,
    An meat unto my man,
    For I will gae to my true-love's gates
    This night, gin that I can.'

216A.2 'O stay at hame this ae night, Willie,
    This ae bare night wi me;
    The best bed in a' my house
    Sall be well made to thee.'

216A.3 'I carena for your beds, mither,
    I carena ae pin,
    For I'll gae to my love's gates
    This night, gin I can win.'

216A.4 'O stay, my son Willie, this night,
    This ae night wi me;

The best hen in a' my roost
Sall be well made ready for thee.'

216A.5   'I carena for your hens, mither,
I carena ae pin;
I sall gae to my love's gates
This night, gin I can win.'

216A.6   'Gin ye winna stay, my son Willie,
This ae bare night wi me,
Gin Clyde's water be deep and fu o flood,
My malisen drown ye!'

216A.7   He rode up yon high hill,
An down yon dowie glen;
The roaring of Clyde's water
Wad hae fleyt ten thousand men.

216A.8   'O spare me, Clyde's water,
O spare me as I gae!
Mak me your wrack as I come back,
But spare me as I gae!'

216A.9   He rade in, and farther in,
Till he came to the chin;
And he rade in, and farther in,
Till he came to dry lan.

216A.10   An whan he came to his love's gates,
He tirled at the pin:
'Open your gates, Meggie,
Open your gates to me,

For my beets are fu o Clyde's water,
And the rain rains oure my chin.'

216A.11 'I hae nae lovers therout,' she says,
'I hae nae love within;
My true-love is in my arms twa,
An nane will I lat in.'

216A.12 'Open your gates, Meggie, this ae night,
Open your gates to me;
For Clyde's water is fu o flood,
An my mither's malison 'll drown me.'

216A.13 'Ane o my chamers is fu o corn,' she says,
'An ane is fu o hay;
Anither is fu o Gentlemen,
An they winna move till day.'

216A.14 Out waked her May Meggie,
Out o her drousy dream:
'I dreamed a dream sin the yestreen,
God read a' dreams to guid!
That my true-love Willie
Was staring at my bed-feet.'

216A.15 'Now lay ye still, my ae dochter,
An keep my back fra the call,
For it's na the space of hafe an hour
Sen he gad fra yer hall.'

216A.16 'An hey, Willie, an hoa, Willie,
Winne ye turn agen?'

But ay the louder that she crayed
He rod agenst the wind.

216A.17   He rod up yon high hill,
An doun yon douey den;
The roring that was in Clid[e]'s water
Wad ha flayed ten thousand men.

216A.18   He road in, an farder in,
Till he came to the chine;
An he road in, an farder in,
Bat neuer mare was seen.

* * * * *

216A.19   Ther was na mare seen of that guid lord
Bat his hat frae his head;
Ther was na mare seen of that lady
Bat her comb an her sneed.

216A.20   Ther waders went up an doun
Eadying Claid's water
Hav don us wrang.

BALLAD NOTES & HISTORY

Dating to the early 19th century, historically this ballad was little known outside of Scotland, where the River Clyde resides. It also goes by the title *The Drowned Lovers*.

SELECTED RECORDINGS

Ewan MacColl, *Clyde's Water* (1956)

Nic Jones, *The Drowned Lovers* (1980)

Martin Carthy & Dave Swarbrick, *Clyde's Waters* (1992)

Kate Rusby, *The Drowned Lovers* (1998)

Anaïs Mitchell & Jefferson Hamer, *Clyde Waters* (2013)

The False Lover
Won Back

Child No. 218: A young man leaves his lover for a fairer maid who lives far away. As he travels to reunite with his new love, his former lover follows him from town to town begging his return. In each town he buys her a gift to bribe her into going home. Finally, he gives in to her persistence, buys her a wedding dress and marries her.

218A.1   A fair maid sat in her bower-door,
          Wringing her lily hands,
          And by it came a sprightly youth,
          Fast tripping oer the strands.

218A.2   'Where gang ye, young John,' she says,
          'Sae early in the day?
          It gars me think, by your fast trip,
          Your journey's far away.'

218A.3   He turnd about wi surly look,
          And said, What's that to thee?
          I'm gaen to see a lovely maid,
          Mair fairer far than ye.

218A.4   'Now hae ye playd me this, fause love,
          In simmer, mid the flowers?

I shall repay ye back again,
In winter, mid the showers.

218A.5 'But again, dear love, and again, dear love,
Will ye not turn again?
For as ye look to other women,
I shall to other men.'

218A.6 'Make your choice of whom you please,
For I my choice will have;
I've chosen a maid more fair than thee,
I never will deceive.'

218A.7 But she's kilt up her claithing fine,
And after him gaed she;
But aye he said, Ye'll turn again,
Nae farder gae wi me.

218A.8 'But again, dear love, and again, dear love,
Will ye never love me again?
Alas for loving you sae well,
And you nae me again!'

218A.9 The first an town that they came till,
He bought her brooch and ring;
And aye he bade her turn again,
And gang nae farder wi him.

218A.10 'But again, dear love, and again, dear love,
Will ye never love me again?
Alas for loving you sae well,
And you nae me again!'

218A.11 The next an town that they came till,
    He bought her muff and gloves;
    But aye he bade her turn again,
    And choose some other loves.

218A.12 'But again, dear love, and again, dear love,
    Will ye never love me again?
    Alas for loving you sae well,
    And you nae me again!'

218A.13 The next an town that they came till,
    His heart it grew mair fain,
    And he was as deep in love wi her
    As she was ower again.

218A.14 The next an town that they came till,
    He bought her wedding gown,
    And made her lady of ha's and bowers,
    Into sweet Berwick town.

BALLAD NOTES & HISTORY

This ballad is rarely found outside of Scotland. Both variants collected by Child were from northern Scotland, though it has found some popularity in the American folk and bluegrass traditions.

SELECTED RECORDINGS

Ewan MacColl & Peggy Seeger,
The False Lover Won Back (1959)

Pat Ryan, *False Lover Won Back* (1977)

Jimmy Hutchison, *False Lover Won Back* (2000)

Frankie Armstrong, *The False Lover Won Back* (2000)

Martin Carthy, *The False Lover Won Back* (2005)

James Harris
(The Daemon Lover)

Child No. 243: James Harris bids his lover, Jane, farewell, and then is off to sea. When Jane receives word that he has died, she marries a carpenter, with whom she has three children. While the carpenter is away, James Harris's spirit returns to woo Jane, promising her love, adventure, and riches if she will sail away with him on his ghost ship. She agrees to go and is never seen again. When the carpenter returns to find his wife is gone he hangs himself, leaving the children orphaned.

243A.1 There dwelt a fair maid in the West,
   Of worthy birth and fame,
   Neer unto Plimouth, stately town,
   Jane Reynolds was her name.

243A.2 This damsel dearly was belovd
   By many a proper youth,
   And what of her is to be said
   In known for very truth.

243A.3 Among the rest a seaman brave
   Unto her a wooing came;
   A comely proper youth he was,
   James Harris calld by name.

243A.4   The maid and young man was agreed,
          As time did them allow,
          And to each other secretly
          They made a solemn vow,

243A.5   That they would ever faithfull be
          Whilst Heaven afforded life;
          He was to be her husband kind,
          And she his faithfull wife.

243A.6   A day appointed was also
          When they was to be married;
          But before these things were brought to pass
          Matters were strangely carried.

243A.7   All you that faithfull lovers be
          Give ear and hearken well,
          And what of them became at last
          I will directly tell.

243A.8   The young man he was prest to sea,
          And forc d was to go;
          His sweet-heart she must stay behind,
          Whether she would or no.

243A.9   And after he was from her gone
          She three years for him staid,
          Expecting of his comeing home,
          And kept herself a maid.

243A.10   At last news came that he was dead
          Within a forraign land,

And how that he was buried
She well did understand,

243A.11   For whose sweet sake the maiden she
Lamented many a day,
And never was she known at all
The wanton for to play.

243A.12   A carpenter that livd hard by,
When he heard of the same,
Like as the other had done before,
To her a wooing came.

243A.13   But when that he had gained her love
They married were with speed,
And four years space, being man and wife,
They loveingly agreed.

243A.14   Three pritty children in this time
This loving couple had,
Which made their father's heart rejoyce,
And mother wondrous glad.

243A.15   But as occasion servd, one time
The good man took his way
Some three days journey from his home,
Intending not to stay.

243A.16   But, whilst that he was gone away,
A spirit in the night
Came to the window of his wife,
And did her sorely fright.

243A.17 Which spirit spake like to a man,
  And unto her did say,
  'My dear and onely love,' quoth he,
  'Prepare and come away.

243A.18 'James Harris is my name,' quoth he,
  'Whom thou didst love so dear,
  And I have traveld for thy sake
  At least this seven year.

243A.19 'And now I am returnd again,
  To take thee to my wife,
  And thou with me shalt go to sea,
  To end all further strife.'

243A.20 'O tempt me not, sweet James,' quoth she,
  'With thee away to go;
  If I should leave my children small,
  Alas! what would they do?

243A.21 'My husband is a carpenter,
  A carpenter of great fame;
  I would not for five hundred pounds
  That he should know the same.'

243A.22 'I might have had a king's daughter,
  And she would have married me;
  But I forsook her golden crown,
  And for the love of thee.

243A.23 'Therefore, if thou'lt thy husband forsake,
  And thy children three also,

I will forgive the[e] what is past,
If thou wilt with me go.'

243A.24   'If I forsake my husband and
My little children three,
What means hast thou to bring me to,
If I should go with thee?'

243A.25   'I have seven ships upon the sea;
When they are come to land,
Both marriners and marchandize
Shall be at thy command.

243A.26   'The ship wherein my love shall sail
Is glorious to behold;
The sails shall be of finest silk,
And the mast of shining gold.'

243A.27   When he had told her these fair tales,
To love him she began,
Because he was in human shape,
Much like unto a man.

243A.28   And so together away they went
From off the English shore,
And since that time the woman-kind
Was never seen no more.

243A.29   But when her husband he come home
And found his wife was gone,
And left her three sweet pretty babes
Within the house alone,

243A.30   He beat his breast, he tore his hair,
            The tears fell from his eyes,
            And in the open streets he run
            With heavy doleful cries.

243A.31   And in this sad distracted case
            He hangd himself for woe
            Upon a tree near to the place;
            The truth of all is so.

243A.32   The children now are fatherless,
            And left without a guide,
            But yet no doubt the heavenly powers
            Will for them well provide.

BALLAD NOTES & HISTORY

The oldest known printing of this ballad is a broadside from 1685 entitled *A Warning for Married Women*, though it was most likely in oral tradition before that. American versions often use the title *The House Carpenter*. In many English variants, the lover's spirit exacts revenge on the woman for not staying faithful to his memory. Irish writer Elizabeth Bowen used the ballad as inspiration for her short story *The Demon Lover*.

SELECTED RECORDINGS

Clarence Ashley, *The House Carpenter* (1930)

A.L. Lloyd & Ewan MacColl, *The Demon Lover* (1956)

Bob Dylan, *House Carpenter* (1961)

Joan Baez, *House Carpenter* (1962)

The Watson Family, *The House Carpenter* (1963)

Dave Van Ronk, *House Carpenter* (1964)

Sweeney's Men, *The House Carpenter* (1968)

Pentangle, *The House Carpenter* (1969)

Tony Rice, *House Carpenter* (1983)

The Handsome Family, *The House Carpenter* (1996)

Tim O'Brien, *Demon Lover* (2001)

Nickel Creek, *House Carpenter* (2002)

Natalie Merchant, *House Carpenter* (2003)

Martin Simpson, *The House Carpenter* (2005)

Frankie Armstrong, *Demon Lover* (2008)

Superwolf, *Demon Lover* (2009)

Alasdair Roberts, *The Daemon Lover* (2010)

Our Goodman

Child No. 274: A man comes home to find several items around the house that suggest another man is there with his wife. When asked about the items, the wife offers various unlikely explanations, hoping to fool him.

274A.1 Hame came our goodman,
    And hame came he,
    And then he saw a saddle-horse,
    Where nae horse should be.

274A.2 'What's this now, goodwife?
    What's this I see?
    How came this horse here,
    Without the leave o me?'
    'A horse?' quo she.
    'Ay, a horse,' quo he.

274A.3 'Shame fa your cuckold face,
    Ill mat ye see!
    'Tis naething but a broad sow,
    My minnie sent to me.'
    'A broad sow?' quo he.
    'Ay, a sow,' quo shee.

193

274A.4   'Far hae I ridden,
    And farrer hae I gane,
    But a sadle on a sow's back
    I never saw nane.'

274A.5   Hame came our goodman,
    And hame came he;
    He spy'd a pair of jack-boots,
    Hwere nae boots should be.

274A.6   'What's this now, goodwife?
    What's this I see?
    How came these boots here,
    Without the leave o me?'
    'Boots?' quo she.
    'Ay, boots,' quo he.

274A.7   'Shame fa your cuckold face,
    And ill mat ye see!
    It's but a pair of water-stoups,
    My minnie sent to me.'
    'Water-stoups?' quo he.
    'Ay, water-stoups,' quo she.

274A.8   'Far hae I ridden,
    And farer hae I gane,
    But siller spurs on water-stoups
    I saw never nane.'

274A.9 Hame came our goodman,
  And hame came he,
  And he saw a sword,
  Whare a sword should na be.

274A.10 'What's this now, goodwife?
  What's this I see?
  How came this sword here,
  Without the leave o me?'
  'A sword?' quo she.
  'Ay, a sword,' quo he.

274A.11 'Shame fa your cuckold face,
  Ill mat ye see!
  It's but a porridge-spurtle,
  My minnie sent to me.'
  'A spurtle?' quo he.
  'Ay, a spurtle,' quo she.

274A.12 'Far hae I ridden,
  And farer hae I gane,
  But siller-handed spurtles
  I saw never nane.'

274A.13 Hame came our goodman,
  And hame came he;
  There he spy'd a powderd wig,
  Where nae wig shoud be.

274A.14 'What's this now, goodwife?
  What's this I see?

How came this wig here,
Without the leave o me?'
'A wig?' quo she.
'Ay, a wig,' quo he.

274A.15 'Shame fa your cuckold face,
And ill mat you see!
'Tis naething but a clocken-hen,
My minnie sent to me.'
'Clocken hen?' quo he.
'Ay, clocken hen,' quo she.

274A.16 'Far hae I ridden,
And farer hae I gane,
But powder on a clocken-hen
I saw never nane.'

274A.17 Hame came our goodman,
And hame came he,
And there he saw a muckle coat,
Where nae coat shoud be.

274A.18 'What's this now, goodwife?
What's this I see?
How came this coat here,
Without the leave o me?'
'A coat?' quo she.
'Ay, a coat,' quo he.

274A.19 'Shame fa your cuckold face,
Ill mat ye see!

It's but a pair o blankets,
My minnie sent to me.'
'Blankets?' quo he.
'Ay, blankets,' quo she.

274A.20   'Far hae I ridden,
And farer hae I gane,
But buttons upon blankets
I saw never nane.'

274A.21   'Ben went our goodman,
And ben went he,
And there he spy'd a study man,
Where nae man shoud be.

274A.22   'What's this now, goodwife?
What's this I see?
How came this man here,
Without the leave o me?'
'A man?' quo she.
'Ay, a man,' quo he.

274A.23   'Poor blind body,
And blinder mat ye be!
It's a new milking-maid,
My mither sent to me.'
'A maid?' quo he.
'Ay, a maid,' quo she.

274A.24   'Far hae I ridden,
And farer hae I gane,

But lang-bearded maidens
I saw never nane.

BALLAD NOTES & HISTORY

This humorous ballad was first printed in the 1776 compilation *Ancient and Modern Scottish Songs*, but is widely believed to be much older. Variants go by many names, including *Four Nights Drunk*, *Seven Drunken Nights*, *Drunkard's Special*, *Cabbage Head*, and *Cat Man Blues*. It is one of the few Child Ballads to enter the African-American folk tradition.

SELECTED RECORDINGS

Coley Jones, *Drunkard's Special* (1929)

Blind Lemon Jefferson, *Cat Man Blues* (1929)

Oscar Brand, *Our Goodman* (1955)

Pete Seeger, *My Good Man (Our Good Man)* (1959)

Sonny Boy Williamson, *Wake Up Baby* (1959)

Ewan MacColl, *Our Goodman* (1961)

The Dubliners, *Seven Drunken Nights* (1967)

Steeleye Span, *Four Nights Drunk* (1971)

Leon Redbone, *Cat Man Blues* (1972)

Kate Rusby, *The Good Man* (2003)

The Mermaid

Child No. 289: Not long after a ship's crew spots a mermaid near the shore—known as an omen of impending doom—the vessel springs a leak and sinks, taking most of the sailors aboard down with it to their deaths.

289A.1 As we lay musing in our beds,
    So well and so warm at ease,
    I thought upon those lodging-beds
    Poor seamen have at seas.

289A.2 Last Easter day, in the morning fair,
    We was not far from land,
    Where we spied a mermaid on the rock,
    With comb and glass in hand.

289A.3 The first came up the mate of our ship,
    With lead and line in hand,
    To sound and see how deep we was
    From any rock or sand.

289A.4 The next came up the boatswain of our ship,
    With courage stout and bold:
    'Stand fast, stand fast, my brave lively lads,
    Stand fast, my brave hearts of gold!'

289A.5 Our gallant ship is gone to wreck,
    Which was so lately trimmd;

The raging seas has sprung a leak,
And the salt water does run in.

289A.6 Our gold and silver, and all our cloths,
And all that ever we had,
We forced was to heave them overboard,
Thinking our lives to save.

289A.7 In all, the number that was on board
Was five hundred and sixty-four,
And all that ever came alive on shore
There was but poor ninety-five.

289A.8 The first bespoke the captain of our ship,
And a well-spoke man was he;
'I have a wife in fair Plymouth town,
And a widow I fear she must be.'

289A.9 The next bespoke the mate of our ship,
And a well-bespoke man was he;
'I have a wife in fair Portsmouth,
And a widow I fear she must be.'

289A.10 The next bespoke the boatswain of our ship,
And a well-bespoke man was he;
'I have a wife in fair Exeter,
And a widow I fear she must be.'

289A.11 The next bespoke the little cabbin-boy,
And a well-bespoke boy was he;
'I am as sorry for my mother dear
As you are for your wives all three.

289A.12 'Last night, when the moon shin'd bright,
    My mother had sons five,
    But now she may look in the salt seas
    And find but one alive.'

289A.13 'Call a boat, call a boat, you little
     Plymouth boys,
    Don't you hear how the trumpet[s] sound?
    [For] the want of our boat our gallant ship
     is lost,
    And the most of our merry men is drownd.'

289A.14 Whilst the raging seas do roar,
    And the lofty winds do blow,
    And we poor seamen do lie on the top,
    Whilst the landmen lies below.

BALLAD NOTES & HISTORY

The Mermaid and its variants are known by a number of names, including *Waves on the Sea*, *The Stormy Winds* and *The Wrecked Ship*. Child's A version was taken from the chapbook *The Glasgow Lasses Garland*, published between 1765 and 1785. The home of the crew members varies from version to version, and has been assigned to nearly every port town in Britain and the east coast of the United States. The earliest recording of the ballad is from 1908, a wax cylinder by Joseph Taylor under the title *Three Times Round Went Our Gallant Ship*.

SELECTED RECORDINGS

Ernest Stoneman & the Blue Ridge Corn Shuckers,
The Sailor's Song (1924)

The Carter Family, *Waves on the Sea* (1962)

Almeda Riddle, *The Nerrimac at Sea* (1972)

Martin Carthy, *The Mermaid* (2006)

Francis James Child

ABOUT THE AUTHOR

JOSHUA HAMPTON is a writer who finds his muse in everything from Anglo-Saxon epic poetry to Appalachian folklore. His work has been featured in *Heroic Fantasy Quarterly*, *Aphelion* and *Mirror Dance*, among others. He is also editor for the English football club Chelsea's stateside newsletter. Joshua lives with his wife, children, two dogs, and the occasional fish near Louisville, Kentucky. His fantasy series *Crowns of Silver & Ash* is available now.

To learn more, visit **www.JoshuaHampton.com**

THANK YOU FOR BUYING THIS BOOK!

I hope you enjoyed *Mad Love, Murder & Mayhem*. If you did, I would kindly ask you to consider leaving a positive review online. Customer reviews (especially those with five stars!) help with sales, and as an independent author every little bit counts. Just a few words is enough. Even if you didn't buy the book online, you can still post your opinion at most retailers if you have an account.

I really appreciate your support and I look forward to reading your feedback.

MORE FROM
JOSHUA HAMPTON

Non-Fiction

The Silver Dagger:
American Murder Ballads

The Wind That Shakes the Barley:
Irish Songs of War & Rebellion

Edgar Allen Poe:
Tales of Mystery & Macabre

Writers, Write!
A Pocket Guide to Media Writing

Fiction

Crowns of Silver & Ash

CPSIA information can be obtained
at www.ICGtesting.com
Printed in the USA
LVHW081102161120
671814LV00024B/506